The
Value Added
Organization

The Value Added Organization

BECOMING A
VALUE ADDED
PEAK COMPETITOR

Tom Reilly

Published by
Motivation Press
St. Louis, MO

Library of Congress Cataloging in Publication Data

Reilly, Thomas P.
  The Value Added Organization—Becoming a
  Value Added Peak Competitor/Tom Reilly
  ISBN: 0-944448-19-4

Other Books by Tom Reilly:
  Value Added Selling
  Value Added Sales Management
  Value Added Customer Service
  Simple Psychology
  Selling Smart
  Crush Price Objections

Acknowledgements

I want to thank my staff, Joann Hamilton, Linda Huizenga, and Charlotte Reilly for their help in producing this manuscript. Mostly, I want to thank them for their commitment to the value added philosophy and for their assistance in helping our company become a value added organization.

Table of Contents

Introduction

Whether you work for a large corporation, small company, school, hospital, police department, non-profit organization, state or federal agency you have two things in common with every other organization and every other employee. You're in business to serve and your organization provides this service with its people. Your organization's effectiveness hinges on your effectiveness. How you approach your career, interact with your peers, and interface with your customers determine the level at which your organization competes and serves. You matter. Welcome to The Value Added Organization—Becoming a Value Added Peak Competitor.

The need to compete and serve effectively has never been greater. Customers want things better, quicker, and cheaper. The pressure to perform is on. The commoditization of products and the convergence of services have sparked an explosion of look-alike products and services. Organizations are scrambling for ways to compete successfully and profitably. Wholesale clubs and super stores have taken the value out of value added reseller and service out of service center. And the Internet has spawned a generation of competitors that specialize in speed and efficiency at lower prices. The competition is fierce.

The most effective way to compete profitably today is to add greater value than the competition. This book is designed to help your organization reach the next level in providing value added solutions for your customers. This book is a catalyst for changing your organization. And you are the change agent. You change your organization by changing yourself. If you change your thinking, you can change your behavior.

I'm less concerned with your title in the organization than I am with your input. Whether you're the chief executive or chief bottle washer, this message is for you. It's a top-down, bottom-up message to help you create meaningful change in you and in your organization. I want to help you lift yourself and your organization to the next level.

Where you work is irrelevant to this conversation. You serve, and your organization competes. Ask your boss if you don't believe me. If you work for a non-profit agency of the government you are still competing. Just ask the motor vehicle registration departments that have privatized. If you are a schoolteacher, your students and their parents have a choice. If you're a physician, your patients want even greater flexibility to choose than they now have. You are competing for customers and clients—whether or not you like it is irrelevant. Every organization competes. If there is no other visible competitor, your competition is your best performance to date. You compete.

This is not Total Quality Management, ISO 9000, or process improvement. I can't help you build a better product unless you are the product. This book is built on a very simple, yet profound, truth: organizational excellence is the natural outcome of individual and team excellence.

The value added philosophy is about doing more of that which adds value to your life and less of that which adds little or no value to your life. This philosophy affects all areas of your life: home, work, play, and community. It affects the way you approach your day and how you pursue your goals.

- In Chapter One I describe value added peak competitors and how their performance lifts their organizations to the next level.

- In Chapter Two I explain the value added philosophy and discuss how everyone in your organization is accountable for customer satisfaction.

- In Chapter Three I challenge you on how you approach your job and how your performance adds value to your organization.

- In Chapter Four I address teamwork and discuss how you, interacting with your peers, create value.

- In Chapter Five I explore how you can interface with customers to provide better service.

- In Chapter Six I discuss after-marketing—the sale after the sale; defensive selling; nailing shut the back door.

- In Chapter Seven I summarize key points from each chapter for your review.

After each chapter I've included a list of thought-provoking questions. These questions encourage you to reflect on your readings and you may even use these as discussion points with your peers or subordinates.

I've written this primer for you—short in length but long in results. It's a quick but powerful read. The premise is simple: you can make this happen. The benefits of reading this book, embracing the value added philosophy, and applying it to your life are straightforward: you will get more out of life by putting more into life; your organization will serve better because you will serve better; your customers, whoever they may be, will get more because you will give more. The strongest benefit that you may experience is how you will feel about yourself after you have practiced this philosophy. You will do more of that which adds value to your life and less of that which doesn't. You will become one of the givers in this world by making a difference in everything you do.

-1-

Value Added Peak Competitors

Since 1981 I've had the privilege of working with some of the best organizations in the world—global leaders in their industries. One of the advantages of working with these organizations is that I learned from them as I taught them. I was their student as well as their teacher. One of the lessons they taught me was how to compete in an industry.

At the most fundamental level of competition is a group of companies I call equalizers or qualifiers. Their primary goal is to close the gap between themselves and other organizations. They want to be as good as the competition. If the competition offers a specific service, these companies will offer that service. If the competition offers a level of quality, the qualifier will also offer that level of quality. The qualifier seeks to close the performance gap between themselves and the rest of the market.

The next higher-level competitor is the differentiator. The differentiator wants to be better than the competition. They want to expand the gap between themselves and others in the industry. If your organization offers follow-up support, the differentiator wants to offer that support and then some. They want to offer better service, better quality, and better employees. Differentiators seek to distance themselves from the rest of the pack to make it easy for customers to choose this solution.

There's a higher-level competitor called the value added peak competitor. Value added peak competitors march to a different drumbeat. Value added peak competitors are those people and organizations that embrace and live the maximum performance philosophy. They expect the best from themselves which enables them to deliver the most value to their customers. They are intrinsically motivated which means they drive from within. There are five characteristics that describe value added peak competitors.

Characteristic #1: Internal Competitive Focus

An internal competitive focus means that they are reaching for something, not running away from something. And what they're reaching for is a higher standard of excellence that is measured against their potential, not against their industry. They judge their accomplishments according to what they're able to deliver. They use internal, not external, benchmarks of excellence. They're aware of industry standards, but they do not internalize another's performance standard as their own.

The directional beacon that helps them navigate their course is internal.

Value added peak competitors are not inhibited by a competitor's successes or intimidated by their failures.

The danger of external benchmarking is that everyone begins to look alike. One definition of a commodity is a product or service differentiated only by its price. When competitor A builds a product that looks a lot like competitor B's product and wraps it in a bundle of services similar to competitor B, customers view this as a commodity. Can you afford for your customers to perceive your product as a commodity?

Because of their internal competitive focus, value added peak competitors have a healthy respect, but not fear, of the competition. "Respect your competitors, but don't hold them in awe or you'll lack the will to beat them." (Ulysses S. Grant) Value added peak competitors are more focused on achieving their potential than defeating a competitor. They march to an internal drumbeat of excellence.

If every competitor, on every playing field looked to the competition for their lead we would never have a Bill Gates, Oprah Winfrey, or Tiger Woods to show us how far humans can travel in pursuit of their dreams.

Characteristic #2: Customer Value Focus

Value added peak competitors define value in customer terms, not seller terms. They view their solution as value received, not just value added. Contrast that with seller-focused value. Seller-focused value is the field-of-dreams business mentality, "If you sell it, they will buy." Or "If you don't sell it, they don't need it." Or as Henry Ford said, "You can have any color car you want as long as it's black." All of these statements reflect the arrogance of seller-focused value.

How do you feel when sellers impose their definitions of value on you? If you're like most people, you resent it. So do your customers.

Because of their customer value focus, value added peak competitors define success as their ability to help customers achieve higher levels of success. They believe that if you help customers achieve high levels of success, you will have all the success that you can handle.

Value added peak competitors are in business to make a difference, not just make a deal. You don't get a lot of promises in business, but I'll make you this one. If your primary focus is, "Where can we make a difference for our customers?" not just "Where can we make a deal?" you'll have all the deals that you can handle because you've had a significant impact on the customer's business.

Value added peak competitors sell to the customer's needs, not necessarily against a competitor's package. If you design a solution to beat a given competitor, the question you may not have asked yourself is, "What's the most we can do for the customer?" Competing against a competitor means that you design a solution to beat their package, but you may not have maximized the value that you can bring to your customer.

Value added peak competitors define value in customer terms; they define success as their ability to help customers achieve higher levels of success; they are more focused on making a difference than just making a deal; and they sell to the customer's needs, not just against a competitor's package.

This customer value focus helps value added peak competitors build trust and rapport with customers. Customers realize that value added peak competitors are in the business of serving, not just selling. Value added peak competitors put the customer's interests first. The customer's needs, wants, and concerns are at the very core of the value added peak competitor's solution.

Like beauty, value is in the eye of the beholder. And value added peak competitors view their solution through the customer's eyes.

Your customer is the reason that you are in business. They are not there to provide you with a job. You are there to provide them with a solution. Your organization gives you this opportunity to serve.

Characteristic #3: Passion for Excellence

Some hear the word excellence and think perfectionism. That's not what I'm talking about here. Perfectionists are never happy with what they've done because nothing is ever good enough. The opposite is true for value added peak competitors. Value added peak competitors are very proud of what they've accomplished. But, they balance that pride with a strong measure of humility that says, "We're not done yet." They accept the reality that everyone can grow, develop, and actualize. Organizations can and do get better. What precipitates your growth is admitting that you're not finished yet.

This passion for excellence comes from their desire to get better. Value added peak competitors challenge the status quo. *Status* comes from that same root word as *static*, which means to stay at rest. There are no sacred cows in these value added peak competitor organizations. They question everything.

Does this policy, procedure, or process add value to what we do, or does it just add cost?

Things that add cost without value diminish your position in the market. They slow you down. It's like driving with one foot on the gas and one foot on the brake. Value added peak competitors are constantly looking for ways to get that foot off the brake so that they can grow to their potential.

It takes courage to be a value added peak competitor. It takes courage to challenge the status quo. It takes courage to swim against the tide. It takes courage to be a leader. Have you ever seen a strong leader without courage?

Value added peak competitors are desperately curious about their potential. As humans, we are born curious about our world. Our destiny is to grow, to develop, to evolve, and to emerge. In fact, one of our most fundamental needs is the need to do a better job today than yesterday, and a better job tomorrow than today.

What is the most rigorous law of our being? Growth. No smallest atom of our moral, mental, or physical structure can stand still a year. It grows—it must grow; nothing can prevent it. (Mark Twain)

Value added peak competitors live this desire for growth and development in the way they approach their jobs. They ask questions like:

- Is this the best I can do with the resources we have available, or can I reach higher?
- Did I bring my "best me" with me today, or did I leave something at the office?
- Is this my best work?

- Would I want to put this work on display for the whole world to view?

Because of this positive addiction to excellence, value added peak competitors reach and stretch. They make habitual what others consider to be a hassle. They have discovered a fundamental truth: there's no traffic jam on the extra mile.

Value added peak competitors have the courage to challenge the status quo and the curiosity to explore their own potential.

Courage, curiosity, pride, and humility: these are great qualities. These are value added peak competitor qualities. Value added peak competitors have a passion for excellence. They're proud of what they've accomplished yet balance it with the humility that they're not yet done.

Characteristic #4: They Add Value With Their People

Value added peak competitors discovered a long time ago that an organization's solution includes three dimensions of value. Dimension number one is your product or service, whether it's a truck, tin cans, office furniture, education, or accounting services. Dimension number two is your organization. This includes financial stability, depth of resources, number of locations, inventory levels, and value added services. Dimension number three is your people. Value added peak competitors understand that people represent the single, unique dimension of value. And they wield this uniqueness for competitive gain.

I can build a product or design a service that looks a lot like yours. If you're in the truck business, I can build a truck that looks so much like your truck that the differences will be imperceptible to most people. I can do this without violating patents. I can bundle a package of services that rivals your services: twenty-four-hour delivery, twenty-four hour per day service, follow-up technical support, financing, road service, and extended warranty.

The unique dimension of value, the one that I cannot copy, is your people. Why? Because there's no commodity in creativity, and there's no traffic jam on the extra mile.

A company president approached me during one of my presentations and said, "Tom, we used to be a peak competitor organization until we lost our best people. Now, we're just like everybody else." People represent the single, unique dimension of value.

Value added peak competitors appreciate their people. They understand that all things being equal, people make a difference. And it is a difference that is not easily copied.

Creativity, initiative, courage, and passion are not commodity characteristics. These are differentiating qualities that build customer loyalty and retention.

Customer loyalty is the behavioral side of customer satisfaction. And customer satisfaction reflects employee satisfaction. Satisfied employees help create satisfied customers. Loyal employees help create loyal customers. A leading predicator of an organization's profitability is customer and employee loyalty.

There are three questions that value added peak competitor employees ask themselves. Question number one is, "Do I add value or cost to our efforts?" This is another way of asking the question, "Am I a cost center or a profit center to my organization?" I'm sure you've figured out that there is no future in being a cost center to your organization.

Question number two is, "Does my energy add to our momentum or does it slow us down?" When you come to work in the morning, your energy does one of two things. It either adds momentum to your team or it serves as a resistance force. You add positive momentum or negative resistance. For which would you rather be known? Which is better for the organization? Which is more productive for the customer? Which is a better way for you to live your life?

Question number three is the fundamental question for value added team members, "What am I personally doing today to add value to our efforts?" If everyone in your organization would ask and answer this question daily you could lift your organization to the next level with your people. A CEO for a major bank once said, "The person or organization that somehow manages to harness the collective genius of his or her employees will blow away the competition."

Characteristic #5: Optimism

Value added peak competitors look to the future through the eyes of an optimist. These are not companies where employees say things like, "Boy, I remember the good old days in this business. Oh baby, those days are gone forever." You don't hear that longing for the past in value added organizations. You know why? These are growing, evolving, and emerging people and organizations.

Value added peak competitors view the future positively because they're planning it to be that way.

Think about it logically. If you measure your performance against your potential; if you define value from the customer's perspective; if you view your success as helping others achieve higher levels of success; if you're more interested in making a difference than just making a deal; if you're energized by your potential and curious enough to pursue it; if you're addicted to excellence in everything you do; if you value your peers, your subordinates, and yourself; if you're committed to adding value, not just creating a job for yourself; and if you believe that people make a difference, how can you say that your best days are behind you?

They must be in front of you! So, when value added peak competitors ask this question, "Are our best days on our horizon, or are they in our wake?" They clearly and confidently respond, "Our best days are in the future, not in the past." Value added peak competitors do not spend much time looking in the rearview mirror. They learn from the past and move on. Too many people are trapped in time. They lock in on yesterday missing today.

It's impossible to get to tomorrow if you're stuck in yesterday. What worked, worked. What failed, failed. Learn from it and move on. To dwell on the past deprives you of the joy of today, and the hope for tomorrow. The reason value added peak competitors are optimistic is that they've learned from the past, they're living in the now, and they're planning for the future.

Chapter Summary

In this chapter I explained the three ways that organizations compete. The first is the qualifier. They choose to be as good as everyone else. They compete by closing the gap between themselves and the rest of the pack. The second is the differentiator. They compete by expanding the gap between themselves and the rest of the pack. They want to be better than everyone else. The third is the value added peak competitor. They compete by asking, "What's the most we can do?" I described five characteristics of value added peak competitors and challenged you with several questions. Now,

I want to challenge you one more time. I want you to see yourself and your organization as value added peak competitors. I'll close the way that I opened this chapter. Your organization can reach heights only to which you and others lift it. Organizational excellence results from individual and team excellence.

Thought Provokers

- Is your organization an equalizer, differentiator, or a value added peak competitor?

- Do you have an internal or external competitive focus?

- Do you have a positive addiction to excellence?

- Do people represent the single unique dimension of value?

- Is there a spirit of optimism in your organization?

- What do you personally need to do to become a value added peak competitor?

-2-

The Value Added Philosophy

In this chapter, I will introduce you to the value added philosophy. I discuss customer satisfaction, who's ultimately responsible for it, and I share with you what customers really want from suppliers. This research is based on our eight-thousand-piece buyer survey. My objective is simple. I want to encourage you to embrace the value added philosophy and internalize the responsibility for creating satisfied customers.

What Is Value

Let's begin with some definitions. Value is really three things. First, it's personal. Like beauty, value is in the eye of the beholder. Some people define value as better quality. Others say, "Value is a cheap price." And yet others say, "Value means that I get what I pay for." The first thing that we can say about value is that it's whatever the customer says it is. This is the value added peak competitors' customer value focus. They define value in customer terms.

If you define value in customer terms, they pay for it with a higher selling price. If you define value in your terms, you pay for it with a higher discount.

Second, there's a perceived aspect to value. Perception is subjective reality. For customers, "What I see is reality for me." It's how they input information and attach meaning to it that forms their perception. And in business, the only reality that exists is in your customer's mind.

Perceived value is the promise that you make; it's the sizzle on the steak. It's the cosmetic and qualitative aspects of what you sell. It gives the customer a warm, fuzzy feeling about your product and company. The promise of value added includes: brand name, your knowledge, and how someone is treated when they call your office. It's how your showroom or offices appear to the customer. It's the condition of your literature. It's your packaging. It's how your products look when they arrive at the customer's location.

These are all examples of perceived value. Perceived value serves an important purpose in business. It fuels the buyer's expectations. Your value added solution becomes the industry benchmark. Buyers perceive greater value in what you deliver and use this standard to judge other suppliers.

The third element of value is performance value. Performance value is your profit impact on the customer's business. It's the steak behind the sizzle. It's the proof behind the promise. It's the quantitative behind the qualitative. And it's the substance behind the style. Performance value is made up of three things. First, acquisition cost—what it costs to buy your product or service. Second, ownership costs—what it costs to own and operate your product. Third, opportunity value—what you empower the customer to do. What does your organization give your customer the opportunity to do tomorrow that they couldn't do today? What problems can they solve tomorrow that they couldn't solve today? How can your customers better serve their customers tomorrow because of your solution?

Perceived value drives customer expectations while performance value affects customer satisfaction.

What Is Value Added

Value added is the difference between raw material input and finished product output. On a practical level, value added is everything your company does to something from the moment you get it until you process it, sell it, service it, and help the customer dispose of it. If you sell lift trucks, value added is everything you do from when you buy the lift truck until you sell it and service it on the back end for the customer. If your company sells a commodity product, it's how you put your fingerprints all over that product from the moment you get it until you sell it and service it. If you're in the service industry, your value added is the way you deliver the service with all the extra special effort you put into it.

Most companies that I have worked with offer their customers significant value added yet much of it is unheralded. A big part of becoming a value added organization is getting credit for all the value added that your company brings to the table.

What Is Customer Satisfaction

What does customer satisfaction mean to you? When I ask this question in seminars I generally hear things like: "Customer satisfaction means that customers come back." "They like what you sell." "They say 'thank you' when they're satisfied." "They smile to let me know that they're happy with what they've bought."

Those are examples of what satisfied customers do. They come back and bring their friends with them. They increase their business with your company or they speak well of your organization.

Customer satisfaction is often expressed as a simple ratio. It's a function of how you perform relative to the customer's expectations.

If your performance is greater than their expectations, you have satisfied customers. On the other hand, if your performance is less than what they expect, you have dissatisfied customers. Customer satisfaction is an attitude that customers form about your total package based on their expectations and experiences with you. When I refer to customer satisfaction, I really go beyond customer satisfaction to include customer loyalty and customer retention.

Customer satisfaction is an attitude. Customer loyalty is a behavior. Exceed customer expectations and they reward you with repeat business.

Customer loyalty and customer retention are behaviors. They are leading predictors of your company's profitability. Customer loyalty means that customers feel satisfaction and you retain the business. The goal in business is to retain the business and grow sales.

What Is Customer Service

How do you define customer service? When I ask that question in seminars I hear a variety of definitions: "Customer service means that if the customer has a problem, we take care of it for them." or "If the customer has a question, we answer it." or "If they have something to be returned, we take care of that also." How does your definition compare to these?

Implicit in each of these definitions is a reactive dynamic. Unless there's a problem, a question, or something to return, the customer doesn't receive customer service. Value added customer service is more than a department. It's not just the three or four people that handle problems. It's a philosophy that everyone in the organization feels and acts responsible for creating satisfied customers.

Who is responsible for creating satisfied customers in your organization? Everyone. It's a proactive philosophy. Don't wait for the customer to experience a problem to give great service. Anticipate, and act in advance. Being proactive means that you never have to say you're sorry to the customer.

Customer service is a philosophy, not a department. Everyone in the organization must feel and act accountable for satisfying customers.

The outcome of this philosophy is a solution to a problem that I've seen in many organizations. Time and again I've heard people say "my" customer or "your" customer. The reality of dealing with customers is that it's not "my" customer or "your" customer. It's "our" customer. Everyone is accountable for creating satisfied customers.

You must embrace this attitude and encourage others to embrace this attitude if your organization is to deliver value added peak competitor service. The result of value added peak competitor service is customer satisfaction, loyalty, and retention. Value added peak competitors exceed customer expectations. They feel and act responsible for creating customer satisfaction. Because of their willingness to take ownership of customer satisfaction, value added peak competitors create loyal customers that return with friends.

Why Companies Fail to Serve Customers Better

Great customer service appears so obvious. Why don't more companies do it? I've studied this issue for years and it boils down to four things.

Number one: some people believe that it takes too much time to deliver better service. In reality it takes more than twice as much time to acquire new customers as it does to retain existing customers. Let me appeal to your common sense. Which do you think takes more time: doing something right for the customer the first time, or doing it over? Does it require more time to meet and exceed your customers' expectations or to generate new business?

One barrier to great customer service is an obsession with pursuing new business. I call this "Pipeline-itis." Companies are so preoccupied with filling the front ends of their pipelines with new business that they often slight their current business. They lose business from the back door while obsessing on bringing in new business through the front door.

Organizations that obsess on new business to the degree that they slight existing customers have revolving doors in the fronts and the backs of their buildings.

Number two: there's a misconception that it's expensive to serve customers. Again, that's false. The latest data estimates that it costs your company ten times more money to get a new customer than to keep an existing customer happy. Another way to view this is that it costs your company one-tenth the cost of securing new business to keep existing customers happy. Gaining new business is important, but not to the extent that you fail to serve existing customers.

Number three: companies don't serve because of ignorance. They don't understand or accept the importance of serving customers. It's difficult to believe that there are companies that still do not recognize the importance of serving customers. Erroneously, they may assume that supplying the product or service is enough.

Number four: apathy. Some companies don't care enough to serve their customers better. These are companies that are in business only to make a sale, not a difference. They view the customer as an account number. The relationship is unimportant to them. This is a prescription for failure.

Danger Signals for Poor Service

How do you know if your company is not providing value added customer service? There are four danger signals.

Number one is internal. When you view the customer as a pain versus a gain, you're on thin ice. Your attitude is the problem. When you perceive the customer as an interruption to your daily routine versus the reason for your daily routine, it's an attitude problem. Customers know when you feel they're an interruption. It's impossible to mask those feelings.

A second danger signal is arrogance. "We're the best. People know who we are. They come to us if they need something." That's true as long as no other competitor attempts to solve those problems for your customer. Value added peak competitors balance their pride with humility. It's their humility that keeps them out of the danger zone.

Every arrogant company is only two bad quarters away from a big case of humility.

A third danger signal is a decline in business. There are noticeable sales decreases in product groups or market niches. This is the customer's not-so-subtle way of expressing their dissatisfaction. They may have found a better way to solve their problem that excludes your company or product and service.

A fourth danger signal is that customers begin to complain about price. Why? Because of a perceived inequity. They feel that they're giving better than they're getting. A failure in service or quality precipitates a price objection from existing customers. Customers that are satisfied with your quality and service rarely complain about price. If you hear price objections from existing customers, it's only the tip of the iceberg.

Understanding the importance of delivering great service and standing vigilant for the danger signals of declining service will keep you on the path of the value added peak competitor.

Barriers to Great Service

I've surveyed several groups of employees with this question, "What are some of the barriers that prevent your company from providing better service for your customers?" Here's what they told me:

Number one: bad attitudes. When everyone fails to embrace the attitude that serving customers is a privilege, not a pain, it shows in their day-to-day treatment of the customers. Customers sense when employees view them as a pain.

Number two: a breakdown in communications—verbal and written. This includes miscommunication among team members or between employees and customers.

Number three: mistakes. Every time I think of this I'm struck by the irony. I'm reminded of how long it takes to do something over. It doesn't take as much time to do it right the first time as it does to do it over.

Number four: time. Time is a precious commodity these days. It seems like we're all so hurried and harried that we don't have time to do all the things that we would like to do. Time pressures are everywhere. There is too much to do and too little time to do it. Couple this with downsizing and reorganizing and most employees have too many things to do in too little time.

Number five: a lack of resources. They told me, "We don't have enough of what we need to do the job that we'd like to do for the customer." This includes computers, inventory, money, and other resources.

Number six: unrealistic expectations. The customer has expectations that nobody could live up to. These may be the result of salespeople over-promising or customers that do not know what is realistic to expect.

Number seven: lack of authority. These are a few things I heard: "I don't have the authority to do the kind of job that I'd like to." "I don't have the authority to create action for the customer." and "It takes too much time for me to get something done because I always need to check with someone else."

Number eight: policies and procedures. Organizations need policies and procedures. They add discipline and form. But when you view policies and procedures as something more than guidelines, they limit you when dealing with customers. Policies and procedures are designed to help you serve better, not slow you down.

Many of the barriers for providing better service are self-inflicted wounds.

Barriers impede customer service. Every company encounters some barriers in their efforts to serve their customers better.

Some of these barriers are self-inflicted wounds: over-promising and under-delivering; embracing the attitude that "this would be a great place to work if it wasn't for the customer"; or a lack of pride in the work one performs.

Other barriers seem more understandable. We live in a world of break-neck speed where there never seems to be enough time to get everything done. Employees work in conditions where they lack the legitimate resources to get the job done. Some employees diligently enforce customer service policies that may have a paradoxical effect on customer satisfaction. The quickest and most effective way to improve your service is to eliminate the barriers that impede your efforts.

What Customers Really Want From Suppliers

The value added philosophy is a double-win because value added peak competitors are committed to equity in their relationships with customers. They give as good as they get. Your goal must be to exceed your customer's expectations. It must be a good deal for both of you.

In our surveys, buyers told us what they really want from sellers. They want more than a cheap price. Only one out of six buyers is a true price shopper. This is the segment of buyers where price is **the** issue. There's another segment where price is **an** issue but not **the** issue. The majority of customers that you deal with want something more than a cheap price. One study found that seventy-two percent of buyers will not shop price if they're convinced that there are value added services in place with the supplier.

Buyers want more than a cheap price: they want to purchase quality products and services from people and companies that care about them.

Buyers told us that they're willing to pay 13.9% more for a better quality product and 9.4% for better service. They appreciate quality and service. That doesn't mean if your service and quality are better that you can charge 23.3% more. But if your quality and service are better, you ought to be able to charge more and get it. Buyers said that they are willing to pay for it.

We asked buyers what they looked for most in a solution. We gave them thirty-six variables to choose from: twelve product attributes, twelve people characteristics, and twelve company attributes. Here is the top ten list:

Number one: customers want to deal with knowledgeable people. They want to do business with salespeople that draw from a wellspring of information to help them solve their problems. Seventy-six percent of value added comes from knowledge-based activities. Your knowledge is value added in the customer's mind. Are you that knowledgeable?

Number two: they want a quality product or service. Buyers want to feel that what they're buying is the best quality product or service that they can afford. Do you provide the best quality product and service?

Number three: they want quick availability. Customers want to be able to buy what they want when they need it. You must have inventory on-hand and be willing to expedite it. Do you have adequate inventory levels and do you respond quickly?

Number four: support after the sale. Everyone wants the security that the supplier will be there for him or her after the sale. They said, "If we spend $100,000 for a piece of equipment, I want to be sure that someone is there to help me take care of it on the back end." How supportive are you after the sale?

Number five: how easy is your company to do business with? Customers want to work with suppliers that make it easy for them to do business with their company. Does your delivery schedule cater to the customer's needs? Does your order entry department make it easy for customers to get things through the pipeline quickly? How easy is it for customers to work with your credit department?

Look for ways to make it easier for your customer to buy from your company.

Number six: customers want performance from your product or service. This determines if they get their money's worth.

Product performance affects customer satisfaction. This is the profit impact you have on their business. What kind of profit impact does your performance have on the customer's business?

Number seven: customers want to deal with people who deliver on their promises. You can promise a lot, but always deliver more than that which you promise. Follow-up builds confidence and credibility. When you exceed their expectations it creates buyer satisfaction. How good are you at follow-up?

Number eight: customers want to deal with people who create results. Do you have the authority, the information, and the ability to create results for your customers? When a customer has a problem, they want someone who will fix the problem, not the blame. Their goal is results. Do you create results for the customer?

Number nine: price. They want equity. Customers pay an amount of money for something and want to receive at least that much in return. Equity feeds satisfaction. What's highly significant about this is that buyers rated eight things as more important to them than a cheap price. Is your solution equitable for customers?

Number ten: overall inventory levels. Customers want to buy from suppliers that have plenty of what they need when they need it. Do you have the depth and breadth of products that customers need? Do you have replacement parts in stock to support the customer? Do you have the maintenance resources to support the customer?

Why Value Added Make Sense for Your Organization

I've talked about what customers want. Now, I'd like to share a couple of thoughts with you about the importance of this double-win philosophy to your company. For a company with average economics, if you offer a ten percent discount on your goods and services, you must increase your volume by one-third to compensate for the lost net profit dollars from discounting. A twenty percent discount means you must double your sales. A thirty percent discount means you must quadruple your sales to compensate for that lost net profitability.

An article that appeared in the Harvard Business Review discussed the impact of an increase in selling price versus an increase in volume. A one percent increase in selling price has three to four times the profit impact on your company as the equivalent one percent increase in volume.

What would happen if your company decided to compete by cutting prices across the board? Consider the impact that would have on the image of your company and the image of your products. How well does that reflect on your company? What is the impact to the trust bond between you and the customer? It's reasonable to assume that customers would ask, "If you can discount now, why haven't you been doing that all along?"

If you compete only on price you may eventually resent the business that you attract.

I've found that when companies choose to compete on a price-only strategy, they resent the business. And when you resent the business, your service falls off, and the customer suffers as a result. The value added philosophy is a double-win philosophy. You're committed to excellence in what you do and equity in your relationships with customers.

Commitment is the degree to which you will inconvenience yourself for something. Value added peak competitors are committed to three things. Number one, they're committed to equity in their relationships with their customers. It's win/win all the way. It must be a good deal for you and a great deal for the customer. Number two, they're committed to excellence in their daily efforts. They take pride in their work. Number three, value added peak competitors have a passion for service. They promise a lot, but always deliver more than what they promise. That's how they create satisfied customers that return and bring friends with them.

Chapter Summary

In this chapter, I introduced you to the value added philosophy. I defined value as three things: it's personal, whatever the customer says it is. There's a perceived aspect of value that gives customers a warm and fuzzy feeling; and there's a performance aspect that has a profit impact on the customer's business.

I defined customer service and customer satisfaction. Customer service is a philosophy in which everyone feels and acts responsible for creating satisfied customers. Customer satisfaction is an attitude that results from your exceeding customers' expectations. Customer loyalty and retention are the behavioral consequences of satisfied customers. And it's loyalty that brings back customers.

I examined some of the reasons why companies fail to serve and the danger signals that indicate your company may not be delivering the kind of service that customers want. I also discussed some of the barriers that inhibit your company from delivering world-class service.

Thought Provokers

- What value added do we offer?
- Do we regularly exceed customer expectations?
- Does everyone feel and act accountable for creating customer satisfaction?
- What are our barriers to better customer service?
- What can we do to make it easier for the customer to do business with us?

-3-

You and Your Career

This chapter is all about you—your career and the difference that you make in your organization. In Chapter One I introduced you to how value added peak competitors view people. They believe that people can and do make a significant difference in an organization. People represent the single, unique dimension of value. With the commoditization of products and the convergence of services, people represent the greatest differentiating potential for organizations.

In this chapter, I examine some of the fundamentals of business and human nature and how these contribute to how you approach your career. Notice I didn't say job, I said career. A job sounds like work—something you must do for a paycheck. A career sounds like passion and avocation—a labor of love.

I will share with you insights from having trained over one hundred thousand employees at all levels in diverse organizations: truck dealers, chemical companies, industrial suppliers, motorcycle manufacturers, agricultural companies, bankers, and health care workers to name a few. I will discuss how your efforts add value to your company's efforts, and how your company's success is tied directly to your personal success. I have a very simple objective in this chapter—to inspire you to seek ways to add value with your performance.

You Own Your Career

Something that has always impressed me about successful people in all walks of life is their personal ownership of their careers. Again, I didn't say jobs; I said careers. It's a personal psychology of, "If it is to be, it's up to me."

Value added peak competitors look inward, not outward, for motivation. They understand that motivation is a do-it-to-yourself kind of thing, an internal not external force. A seminar attendee told me that his objective for attending the training was to learn how to motivate himself because he had a terrible manager. His manager didn't know how to motivate him. I looked at this gentleman and thought, "He doesn't grasp the essence of motivation."

Motivation is a do-it-to-yourself thing. It's engaging your internal kick-starter.

Motivation is a very personal thing. It's something we do to and for ourselves. Everyone is motivated. We're just motivated to do different things. Motivation comes from within the individual, not from outside. As a self-employed individual for the past 20-plus years, I've had to embrace this

38

philosophy to start, operate, and grow two successful businesses. And I've seen this same level of career ownership at all levels in other organizations. For example,

- Auto mechanics invest $20,000-$30,000 in the tools of their trade. A tool supplier may come around once a month to take money out of their paycheck to pay for this investment. These mechanics invested in themselves and in their careers.

- I've met salespeople who spend $4,000 or $5,000 on laptop computers, printers, and modems to do a better job for their customers. This is another career investment. No one told them to do it. They did it for themselves and for their customers.

- There are nurses who take the initiative to go back to school because they want to stay current with all the changes in their profession. This is an investment in their personal knowledge. They take their careers seriously.

- Technicians study service manuals and training videos at home to build their knowledge base. This increases their value to the company and service to the customers. Mostly, it helps them do the quality of work they're capable of delivering. I call this professional pride.

- Customer service reps attend business-writing classes because they feel that skill needs development. They're filling a skill gap. They recognize that this gap may hold them back. They are committed to their careers.

- Secretaries take word processing courses on their own so they can do a better job at work during the day. They bring greater value to the job.

- First-level managers pay for self-development training out of their own pockets because they realize that "my career is my career, and nobody in this world is more responsible for it than I am."

Did you notice that in each of these examples the employee felt ownership and took responsibility for their careers. Nobody told them to do these things. They did them on their own initiative. More importantly, they did it for themselves. They were the primary beneficiaries of these investments. The company and the customers gain from these initiatives. But, it's the employee who gains the most. Why? Because they invested in their careers. It makes them more valuable to their companies and competitive in the market. When you invest this way, you do it for you. Others seek you out because you are a valuable commodity.

Ninety percent of your success comes from things that you control and the decisions that you make.

Personal ownership of your career begins with the ninety percent rule. Over the years I've surveyed people and compiled a list of the things that account for career success. Ninety percent of the things that account for success in any career are things over which people have control. Things like: attitude, knowledge, integrity, enthusiasm, pride, passion, communica-

40

tion skills, personal organization, good relationships, team attitude, and initiative. These are things that you control. Many people have told us that they like this ninety percent rule because it gives them ownership of their careers and autonomy in pursuing excellence in their jobs.

By owning your career you exhibit a characteristic that all successful people demonstrate: personal initiative. Initiative is your internal kick-starter. It's that stuff you do without somebody telling you to do it. It's the habit of going the extra mile.

The examples that I cited earlier were people who invested in themselves because of personal initiative. They invested in their own growth and development. They invested in their careers.

Once you accept that no one is more responsible for your career than you are, it's easier for you to take the initiative to start living that philosophy.

Value added peak competitors have discovered that there's no traffic jam on the extra mile. They may not possess superhuman talent but they have accepted full responsibility for their careers and have taken the initiative to do something about it. They make it a habit of doing what others consider a hassle. Successful people at all levels and in all fields do what others fail to do.

People Work for More Than the Money

In all my years of business and from all my studies in psychology, there's one thing about the human condition of which I'm absolutely certain: everyone works for something other than just money. We draw two types of rewards from the work that we do. We experience intrinsic satisfaction for having done the job well. These are the warm and fuzzy feelings of knowing that you've performed at your best. This is the inner applause. You feel good about your performance.

The other rewards are extrinsic: the accolades, the benefits, the pay, the recognition, the respect of peers, and the feeling that you're a part of something bigger than yourself. These rewards come from outside of you.

If people only worked for the money, they would rob banks or choose get-rich-quick schemes because that's where all the money is, right? People work for more than just the money. They want to feel good about the work they do. Value added peak competitors survive on the money but they thrive on the intrinsic satisfaction from doing good work. They thrive on fun, and doing the job well is fun. There's pleasure in that. It satisfies their professional curiosity. Every serious person I've met in business is curious about his or her potential. They ask, "I wonder how good I am in my field."

Value added peak competitors are desperately curious about their potential and motivated to satisfy this professional curiosity.

The inner applause of knowing that you've done your best work makes you feel like a professional in your field. It's a professional pride in your daily efforts. P. R. I. D. E. is a great acronym to describe the satisfaction you feel when you do your best work:

PROFESSIONAL RESULTS IN DELIVERING EXCELLENCE.

Martin Luther King, Jr. wrote, "If a man is called to be a street sweeper, he should sweep streets even as Michelangelo painted, or Beethoven composed music, or Shakespeare wrote poetry. He should sweep streets so well that all the hosts of heaven and earth will pause to say, here lived a great street sweeper who did his job well."

It's intrinsically satisfying to explore your creativity. It's exciting to have the autonomy or freedom to make decisions that affect your career. It's exhilarating to think you're at the top of your game. In fact, I'd be willing to bet that if you looked back at a time in your life where you felt most alive and most successful, it was when you held yourself to a higher personal standard of excellence. Your daily mantra was, "I'm better than that."

Intrinsic satisfaction is the feeling that what you do is meaningful and makes a difference in this world. Everyone wants to be a part of something bigger than themselves. Everyone wants to contribute. It feels good to do something that you know is important to someone else.

Work also offers practical reinforcement—the pay and the benefits. And this is important stuff. You need the money and benefits to pay the bills. You deposit this extrinsic motivator, the paycheck, in your bank account.

You deposit these intrinsic motivators in your emotional bank account: feeling good about your work; taking pride in your efforts; exploring your creativity; feeling in control of your destiny; making a difference with your job; and being an important part of something bigger than yourself. These motivators are priceless.

Your work satisfies two levels of needs. On one level, you earn money that enables you to take care of the necessities and the niceties of life. On another level, you work for the satisfaction of exploring your creativity and your potential.

It feels good when your company recognizes your efforts and rewards you for them. It feels great when you draw on the intrinsic satisfaction, the inner applause, for having done a great job. You are your number one coach, cheerleader, and fan. The inner applause satisfies the coach, cheerleader, and fan. It's good to hear it from others. It's great to hear it from

44

within. Ultimately, you must satisfy yourself with your efforts because you are your own motivator.

How Do You Personally Add Value

How do you bring value with your job? Are you a cost center or a profit center for your organization? Everyone in your organization either adds value or they add cost to your company's solution for the customer. There's no security these days in being a cost center. There's only security when you add value.

What are you doing today to add value to your organization's efforts? This is another way of asking, "Are you a profit center or a cost center to your organization?"

Value added peak competitors seek ways to add value because that's the way they live their lives. They naturally put forth extra effort. Excelling is a habit for them. An effective way to add value is to identify "impact areas" where you can make a difference for the customer or for your company. Your behavior has a positive impact on your company's performance and how you treat customers.

A few years ago I was in Sacramento working with an equipment dealer. I assembled a group of employees and asked them, "How do you personally add value?"

One of the mechanics said, "On every piece of equipment that I work on, I perform a five-point safety check just to

45

make sure that everything that leaves my repair bay is safe for our customers to operate."

One of the salespeople in the group heard this and asked, "Do you perform that test on everything?"

The mechanic said, "Yeah."

And the salesman said, "I can sell that this afternoon."

A customer service rep told me that every Monday morning she checks her backorder reports and gets updated shipping information. She contacts her customers and gives them the new information. She said, "When I contact them, they call it service. When they call me, it's a complaint."

A manager told me that he added value with the amount of time he spent face-to-face with customers. He could get things done. By having his ear that close to the ground, he was able to prevent many of the fires that other companies had to fight.

A salesperson told me that she added value with her twenty-four hour per day accessibility to customers. She gave them her home phone number, beeper number, cell phone, and inside contacts. She made sure that her customers were never out of touch.

An accounting person told me that she saw her role as building bridges with customers, not walls to keep the bums out.

She looked for ways to help customers qualify for credit versus disqualify them.

A driver told me that he went the extra mile for the customer by adjusting his route to deliver when it was more convenient for the customer. He said, "I want to make it easy for our customers to receive our deliveries. Other drivers won't do that." This driver made it a habit to do what others viewed as a hassle.

There's a fundamental similarity in the way each of these employees added value. They put the focus on the customer and asked themselves an important question, "What can I do today to make a difference for our customers?" Each of them had an impact on the customer's life. This added-value approach reflected positively on their companies.

You could lift your organization to the next level if everyone in your organization asked and answered this question daily, "What am I personally doing today to add value to our efforts?"

Value added peak competitors add value with their positive habits. They make it a habit to go the extra mile. They make it a habit to add value to their organization's solution. They make it a habit to go the extra distance for their customers. Can you imagine the impact on your company if everyone did this? What would it mean to the quality of your products, the quality of your service, and the impact on your customer?

47

Value Added Affects All Areas of Your Life

Do you see yourself as a value added peak competitor? Do you make it a habit to go the extra mile? Do people say you're a giver or a taker?

The value added philosophy affects your life in many ways. Once you begin seeing yourself as someone who contributes value, it spills over into other areas in your life. You manage your time more effectively. You readily identify those things that drain your productivity and eliminate them. Some people call these time wasters. I call them time piranhas. They chew away at your effectiveness and your efficiency. They prevent you from accomplishing great things. They distract you.

Because of this value added philosophy you become more selective in your activities. You do more of that which adds value to your life and less of that which adds cost to your life.

As a believer in the value added philosophy, you approach your relationships differently. Whether it's at work, at home, or at play, you seek ways to add value to those relationships. You look for ways to build people up, not break them down. You want to add positive energy to your relationships.

Those who believe in the value added philosophy are generally involved in their communities. They recognize the importance of giving back. They embrace the philosophy that we are brought into this world to leave a bigger woodpile than the one we found. They add value to their communities.

Value added peak competitors are go-getters. They belong to organizations and you typically see them in leadership positions. They're uncomfortable on the sidelines. They thrive on being a part of something bigger than themselves. They give back—doing for and with others. Value added peak competitors are involved.

As humans, we move in the direction of our thoughts. At the core of motivated behavior are values. What you value and how you think determine your behavior, and your behavior determines your effectiveness.

When you conceive of yourself as a giver you automatically look for ways to contribute value. Compare that to the taker. Everyone knows a taker: a peer, a boss, a spouse, a child, a customer, or even a friend. This is the person who defines success as their ability to get as much as they can from others for themselves. Others recognize it and resent it.

Value added peak competitors find it difficult to conceive of the taker lifestyle. They combine their desire to excel with a passion for serving. The net result is that they add value in everything that they do. They live this philosophy daily, at home and at work. It would be unnatural for them to live any other way.

Do you see yourself as a value added peak competitor? Do you find yourself adding value in all that you do? Have you embraced the attitude of giving versus taking? Are you willing to leave a little bigger woodpile than the one that you found in this world?

Chapter Summary

My message in this chapter was simple: people can and do make a difference. As a value added employee you make a difference. I discussed some of the realities of operating in a value added organization. One reality is that you alone are responsible for your career. If you accept this reality, it's easier for you to take the initiative to reach higher levels in your career. Those who believe that someone else is responsible for their success stumble miserably throughout most of their professional lives. They wait and hope for others to do for them what they must do for themselves.

Another reality is that people work for more than just the money. Everyone wants to be part of something bigger than themselves. Everyone enjoys hearing that inner applause. Everyone wants to feel that what he or she does counts; that it's meaningful; and that they're making a difference in this world.

A third reality is that as a value added team member, you're either a cost or a profit center to your organization. I challenged you with a question, "What are you personally doing today to add value to your company's efforts?"

The value added philosophy transcends your career. It affects every area of your life: work, home, and community. As you add value in one area of your life it will have an outward rippling effect in other areas.

At the beginning of this chapter I drew a parallel between value added peak competitor organizations and their people. Now I want to take it a step further. Value added peak competitor organizations are great because of their people. Your role in this effort makes your company successful. Your organization's success depends on your success as an individual and as a leader: your passion, your initiative, and the value that you bring to the table. How will you add value to your company?

Thought Provokers

- Do you own your career?

- Who is ultimately responsible for your success?

- Do you work for more than just the money? If so, What?

- Can you hear the inner applause when you work at your potential?

- How do you personally add value to your organization's solution?

- Do you see the link between your performance and the level at which your organization competes?

-4-

You and Your Peers

In Chapter Three I discussed how you approach your career and how your value added affects your organization's performance. In this chapter I will discuss how you, interacting with your peers and co-workers, create the value added team. A team is only as strong as its weakest member. I want to help your organization build a strong, value adding, customer serving, quality enhancing, and mutually respecting work culture. How you interact with each other defines your work culture.

Specifically, I will discuss the importance of internal customer service and the impact of this synergy on your business culture. I will talk about when teams fail and when teams succeed and what you can do to become a value added peak competitor teammate.

Your energy either adds to your team's momentum or it serves as a resistance force.

Everyone Has a Customer

Whether it's manufacturing, distribution, or the service industry, a fundamental business reality is that everyone in the organization has a customer—either external or internal. Who are your internal customers?

External or traditional customers are those with whom you deal face-to-face, on the telephone, through electronic commerce, or behind-the-scenes. These are people outside of your company that pay for your goods and services. Internal customers are other employees in your organization with whom you interact. For example, bosses interacting with subordinates have an internal customer relationship.

Everyone in every organization has a customer—either external and/or internal.

Human resources may have as its internal customers most other departments in the organization. The information systems department may serve the marketing department. The service department is generally the internal customer of the parts department. Customer service is the internal customer of the sales force, and so on.

If you work for a government agency and interface with the general public the general public are your external customers. Your peers, other departments, and sister agencies may be your internal customers. Teachers, do you view students as customers? Physicians, do you view patients as customers or interesting cases?

There are two corollaries that accompany this fundamental business reality. Corollary number one is that the way you treat each other has an outward, rippling effect on how you treat your external customers. A second corollary is that you can only treat your external customers to the degree to which you treat your internal customers.

The way you treat each other defines the culture of your organization. When team members treat each other with respect they will treat their external customers with respect.

Customer satisfaction mirrors employee satisfaction. Satisfied, happy employees create satisfied, happy customers. A great rule of thumb for any business is to treat each other with the same respect that you feel your best customers deserve.

There's a special dynamic at work in every organization as team members work together. It's called **synergy**. Synergy describes the concept, "we is greater than me." Our collective effort is greater than the sum total of our individual efforts. Two people pulling together bring more to the table than the sum total of the energy that each of them brings to the table. It's possible for two people to work just as hard individually or independently and not have the same impact as they could working together.

We call this the silo effect: individuals or departments working so independently of each other that it may seem they're working for different organizations. I've worked for clients where each department acted as if it were an independent entity—a company unto itself. In some organizations there is fierce competition among departments. One works to upstage the other. Who benefits from that?

With all the competition you have outside of your walls, do you really need departments competing with each other? We is greater than me. When everyone in the organization embraces the attitude that everyone serves someone, either internal or external, and behaves that way, you create a culture of serving that increases customer satisfaction. Your mutual respect and trust for each other spills over in the way you treat your customers.

When Teams Fail

Value added peak competitors believe that serving customers is a team sport. Some teams succeed and others fail. Successful teams offer value added solutions that satisfy customers' needs while contributing to their organization's effectiveness. These results-oriented work groups offer team members the opportunity to feel like they are an important part of something bigger than themselves.

Teams fail when selfishness or personal interests overshadow the team's efforts. Hoarding vital information weakens the team spirit and its effectiveness. When one department hoards information to the detriment of another, it's difficult to serve customers effectively. It impedes the organization's efforts. Selfishness is also a problem when one team member is more focused on creating a job for himself than cooperating with the team to serve customers better.

Teams fail when there's too much me and too little we.

Teams fail when there's active or passive sabotaging of their efforts. Passive sabotaging is letting others fail when you could step in to help. This sin of omission hurts the team spirit and effort. Active sabotaging is creating barriers that prevent someone from doing the kind of job they can do. Spreading gossip and rumors that hurt team members ultimately hurt the saboteur. Others lose trust in this person.

Teams fail when team members sharp-shoot or discount another's ideas. It's easy to criticize another person's idea. It's an act of teamwork to support them. You're either building up or breaking down your teammates.

Attributing motives to another person's behavior is another reason teams fail. It's difficult to know what's in another's heart—why someone does something. Second-guessing a team member's motivation is a waste of your energy and it hurts the team dynamic. It's a more positive use of energy to think well of teammates and assign benign motives to their efforts.

57

Another reason that teams fail is mission creep. Mission creep is losing sight of the mission. "Why are we really doing this?" When you find your team wandering aimlessly trying to get back on track you're experiencing mission creep. You've lost your focus.

When you review the primary mission of most businesses it's to make a difference for the customers, not just a deal. When you lose sight of the mission to bring maximum value to the customer, mission creep has set in. When employees get so bogged down in the details of their day-to-day experiences that they forget why they are in business, to serve customers, mission creep has set it.

Teams also fail because of infrastructure problems. If you lack the resources, the systems, or the time to perform your job the way it should be done, your team will fail. Even successful teams struggle at times. How they deal with the struggles, the obstacles, and the temporary detours determines whether or not they will be successful in their efforts.

With all the competition that your company faces on the streets, you do not need more competition within your walls. You and your peers are on the same team. You are not the enemy. When one team member fails the team is weakened. You are only as strong as your weakest teammate. How you support each other defines the character of your team.

What are you doing today to add value to your team?

When Teams Succeed

On a more positive note teams succeed under these conditions. First, there must be mission clarity. Everyone on the team must understand the mission, what's expected of them, and be committed to that mission. This is management's responsibility to articulate clearly to employees their mission. When employees embrace the mission it becomes a unifying goal for the entire team. Teams function well when everyone knows what's expected of them and commit to that mission.

Teams function best when the team members remain focused on their mission and do not allow themselves to be distracted along the way. They lock in on the mission and lock out the distractions. Planning helps teams maintain their focus. The plan is the team's road map for success. It includes the objectives, strategies, and tactics to accomplish the mission. It's the link between dreams and reality.

Teams work when there's balanced participation by everyone on the team. The failure of one person on the team to pull his load means that others must pick up the slack. On the other hand, all team members pulling together is a powerful source of energy.

When everyone shares in the decision process, they are contributing their ideas to the team. They are an important part of the process. It may not result in a committee decision, but everyone has input on that decision. This builds commitment to the ultimate decision.

Teams work well when there are clearly defined roles utilizing everyone's strengths. The collective, unique strengths of the team members make the team concept so powerful. We is greater than me.

Every team must have a strong leader. This is someone who can make the tough calls. Typically, it's a team member that everyone respects. The team leader influences the actions of the team. Colin Powell said this about leadership, "It's the art of accomplishing what the science of management says is possible." Team leaders help others see what's possible.

There must be a team attitude or a team environment. This means that individual team members must be willing to subordinate their egos for the greater good of serving their customers. After all, that is the mission.

Teams work well when there's a mutual trust and respect for other team members. Trust is the currency of all great relationships. Respecting fellow team members builds this trust. When people trust each other, like each other, and want to work together, they figure out the rest.

Frank, open communication among team members is critical for the team's success. Team members must feel that they can speak openly to other team members. If there's a problem, they must discuss it. The team leader sets the tone for this openness.

Part of the team attitude is a problem-solving environment. This is where you're focused on fixing the problem, not the blame. The most important thing to accomplish is resolution of a problem, not finger-pointing at each other. Stay mission-focused.

There are some ground rules that provide structure for the team to work well. Everyone on this team has value. One team member is no more valuable than another. Everyone brings a unique source of information, attitude, and skill level. Everyone on this team has value and you must value each other. No one member is above or greater than the team.

Teams succeed when there's synergy: a we-is-greater-than-me group attitude.

Attack problems, not people. If there's a problem to be fixed, go after that problem, not the people involved. Fix the problem, not the blame. Team members are more likely to participate when they realize blame is not on the agenda. Blame is a negative use of the team's energy. If it is a problem that involves customers, they do not want to know which team member is at fault. Customers want the problem fixed.

Listen fully to another's ideas without prejudging them or allowing personal biases to influence you. Other people's ideas have merit. Give others the opportunity to express themselves fully. Demonstrate the open-mindedness you expect. No one has a monopoly on great ideas. You may find in a team member's thoughts the seed of a greater idea and build on it with your own. That's the essence of teamwork. You build on each other's strengths while working toward a common goal.

Never second-guess another person's motivation. This is one of the most common reasons teams fail. One team member believes that another member has a hidden agenda. Assume positive motives by fellow team members. Give them the benefit of the doubt.

Teams work well when management provides clear access to information. Everyone involved must share information with peers. There's no holding back. Share openly. It's the synergy of one team member working selflessly with another team member toward a common goal that captures the spirit of teamwork.

Strong teams are composed of strong team members led by a strong leader. This vital team dynamic—collective strength— is a powerful force. This strength resonates in a clarity of and commitment to a mission; mutual respect and support; and balanced participation. It germinates from a simple belief that everyone has value. The net result is a we-is-greater-than-me team attitude.

Teams succeed or fail on the backs of team members. As a value added team member, your efforts influence the success of your team.

Many of the characteristics that I've used to describe value added peak competitors are the same characteristics that make you a great team player: courage, creativity, initiative and empathy. You demonstrate courage when you challenge the status quo and groupthink. This is a phenomenon where everyone in the group locks in on an idea and is unable to challenge it. Everyone thinks alike. Someone must step forward and challenge the group to think outside of the box.

It takes courage to make the tough calls and the tough decisions. It takes courage to step in when the group needs leadership to keep them focused on the mission. It takes courage to challenge the group to stretch and to reach for a higher standard of excellence.

Your creativity stimulates you to pursue new ways to solve old problems. It opens your mind to hear the ideas of other team members. Your initiative paves the way for you to feel responsible for the group's successes and failures. It drives you to seek ways to add greater value to the team—to be a giver, not a taker.

As a team member, your empathy spurs you to reach out to another team member who is struggling and needs help. It means that you will listen to other team members and attempt to involve them. Your empathy helps you to support an open forum where other team members feel free to express their ideas. It signals to others that you are open to their feedback and suggestions.

63

Courage, creativity, initiative, and empathy: these are characteristics of value added peak competitor team members.

Imagine how it would feel to have a teammate who listens without judging, encourages your ideas, has the courage to speak up when it's right to do so, and whose positive energy adds to the team's momentum. You can be this team leader if you choose to be. It's up to you.

Chapter Summary

In this chapter I discussed a fundamental business reality: everyone in the organization has a customer, internal or external. I discussed two corollaries associated with this reality. First, you treat your external customers only to the degree to which you treat each other. Second, how you treat each other has an outward, rippling effect on the way you treat your external customers. Customer satisfaction mirrors employee satisfaction.

I discussed when teams fail and when they succeed. Teams fail when there's too much "me" and not enough "we." Teams succeed when members work diligently and cooperatively toward a common goal.

I discussed characteristics of value added peak competitor team members: courage, creativity, initiative, and empathy. I challenged you to become this kind of teammate.

The ideas in this chapter challenge you to continue to build an environment where we is greater then me—an environment where teams work and egos are put on hold for the greater good of serving customers. Teamwork is the synergy of you interacting with your peers and treating each other with mutual respect. This synergy contributes to the value added solution your company offers your customers.

Remember, organizational excellence is a function of how you individually bring value to the table; and how you and your peers, operating as a team, bring value to the table. Your company's success depends upon the success of its teams.

Thought Provokers

- Who are your internal customers?

- Does your organization have a "we is greater than me" attitude?

- Does your energy add positively to your team's energy?

- Is the silo effect a problem in your organization?

- Do you believe that there is a team atmosphere in your organization?

-5-

You and Your Customers

In this chapter I will discuss your relationship with customers and how this affects your company's value added solution. Specifically, my objective is to encourage you to embrace the attitude of gratitude that serving customers is a privilege, not a pain.

Think about a situation where you were the customer and you were treated poorly. For example, you may have been at your doctor's office, a department store, an auto dealership, or the motor vehicle registration office.

How did you feel as a customer? Were you frustrated, disappointed, or angry? Did you tell your friends and peers about the poor treatment you received? Consider how much money this company spends on advertising to draw people into their store? The positive effects of those advertising dollars are negated by that one bad experience.

When customers have a bad experience with a company they tell an average of twenty-six people about that bad experience. What impact does negative word-of-mouth advertising have on sales? Your company can spend millions of dollars to promote a special image to customers and to attract them to your business.

However, it's the customer's real life experience with your company that brings him back. Your company's sales force sells the first experience to the customer. How you and your peers treat the customer bring him back.

I'd like you to consider another scenario. Again, you're the customer. But this time you are treated fairly. In fact, you're treated well. What did that person do that really made a difference?

How do you feel now? Let's contrast those emotions with the first scenario where you were treated poorly. What will you tell people now? Do you plan to go back? The goodwill that was created in the second scenario is a bargain compared to how costly it was to lose it in the first scenario.

The things that irritate you as a customer irritate your customers. The things that satisfy you as a customer satisfy your customers.

Did you notice that the things that frustrate you as a customer are the same things that frustrate your customers? The things that bring you back are the same things that cause your customers to return. The central theme of these two scenarios is empathy. You experienced what it's like to be a customer, from the customer's point of view.

Customer-izing

Customer-izing is learning to think as your customers think. It's defining value in their terms. In Chapter Two, I discussed value and pointed out that some people define value as quality. Others define it as good service. Some people define it as quick delivery. Other people define it as support. And, yes, even some define it as a cheap price.

Customer-izing is understanding your customer's unique definition of value. It's viewing your product or service as value received, not just value added. Thinking in customer terms requires empathy. Customer-izing is operating with a customer-oriented business philosophy. A customer-oriented business philosophy puts the spotlight on the customer.

Customers are your reason for being. They are not the enemy. Customers are the reason you get a paycheck. They are the reason that you go to work everyday.

The Customer's Bill of Rights is a training exercise that I conduct in our seminars. The Customer's Bill of Rights is the answer to this question, "What do our customers have a right to expect when they buy from our company?" I want to share

with you a Bill of Rights from a small company I worked
with.

- Our customers have a right to expect a quality product
  and prompt service every time they call us;

- Our customers have a right to expect accuracy in our
  quoting and our billing procedures;

- Our customers have a right to expect knowledgeable
  salespeople with no hassles;

- Our customers have a right to expect strong technical
  support on the back end;

- Our customers have a right to expect us to do it right the
  first time, every time.

- Signed,

- The Employees of XYZ Organization

Its brilliance is its simplicity. The employees that deliver the
service, not management, constructed this Customers' Bill of
Rights. The owner of that company is a pretty smart guy. He
knew what he had and took it to a local print shop. They created two posters: one to hang in the office and one for the
shop wall. The first day the poster hung on the office wall,
someone from the shop saw the poster and said, "Hey, look
at Idea Number Three. That was my idea." He signed the Bill
of Rights. A few minutes later a secretary signed the Bill of
Rights. After that, one of the customer service reps signed it.
By the end of the day, every employee in that small organization signed that Bill of Rights. They did this unprompted.

What do you think about their level of commitment for serving customers?

Many companies with whom I've worked have used this Bill of Rights several ways. One company put it on their web site. Another company printed it on the back of their business cards. And still another company created a Bill of Rights brochure to distribute to their customers. This is a great exercise for you to conduct with all of your employees. Involve everyone. Record their answers and consolidate them to create the Bill of Rights. The only thing that limits your usage of the Bill of Rights is the edge of your imagination.

Serving Is a Privilege, Not a Pain

Over the years I've met thousands of people that embrace the attitude of gratitude, that serving customers is a privilege, not a pain. The opportunity to serve your customers is the reason that you go to work every day.

I had been on the road for several days, and I was staying at an Anchorage hotel. I ordered room service. When the room service person delivered my meal he noticed that I had a bag of laundry in the corner of my room.

He said, "Sir, is that laundry going downstairs?"

I responded, "Sure."

He said, "Let me take that for you."

I said, "Don't worry about it. I've got to go past the bell stand myself later. I'll drop it off then."

"Oh, no sir. Please let me do it. It would be my privilege."

And with that, he grabbed the bag and left quickly without looking for a tip. He was someone who clearly lived the attitude of gratitude. He saw an opportunity to serve and he seized it. For him, serving customers was a privilege, not a pain. His actions spoke louder and more effectively than any advertising message his company could have designed.

Because of this attitude of gratitude, value added peak competitors exhibit high levels of personal initiative in three distinct areas with customers.

First, value added peak competitors are willing to go the extra mile. In fact, they make it a habit of going the extra mile. They do their jobs and then some. They go the extra steps in getting something done. They put forth the extra effort in doing things. Listen to those key words: **extra** mile, **extra** steps, **extra** effort. In other words, they do that little bit of **extra**. The difference between ordinary service and extraordinary service is that little bit of **extra** that you put into it.

For example, when value added peak competitor employees hear a problem, a question, or a challenge from a customer, they ask themselves, "How far can I take this myself before I bounce it to someone else?" If the attitude of service is in place, the behavior naturally follows. They naturally look for ways to solve the problem before they hand it off to someone else. Going the extra mile is second nature to them.

The second example of high levels of personal initiative is the habit of being proactive. Being proactive is acting in advance. It's doing something without someone telling you to do it.

Being proactive with customer service means never having to say you're sorry to a customer.

When I was a salesman a purchasing agent said to me, "Tom, one of the most important things that you can do is to stay ahead of the curve and keep me out of trouble." His advice was for me to be proactive in how I approached my job so that I could make him look good to his internal customers.

Being proactive is the habit of anticipating and taking action. It's preventing fires versus putting out fires. It's acting before something becomes a problem situation. When taking initiative you may find that much of the great work you perform goes unrecognized by others because you're preventing a fire, not putting out a fire. You may not get all the external credit that you feel you deserve. But you feel it on the inside. You hear the inner applause for a job well-done.

The sales rep who has a problem with invoicing and fixes it before the customer discovers the problem is delivering proactive service.

It's the customer service rep who anticipates a shortage and takes the initiative to contact the customer to inform him that there may be a future problem. The customer service rep may ask the customer, "Would you like to deal with this in advance and place your order?"

It's the mechanic who works on a piece of equipment and notices that something else should be done. He takes the initiative to fix it versus waiting for someone to say, "Why didn't you fix that?"

The habit of being proactive distinguishes value added peak competitors from the rest of the crowd. Value added peak competitors take charge.

Sometimes it's better to ask forgiveness than permission. This is another way of saying, "Make a decision and act." Take the lead in serving customers.

The third way value added peak competitors live this high level of initiative is that they perform tasks at mach one response time. Mach one is the speed of sound. That's fast!

Time is **the** competitive advantage of the twenty-first century. Value added peak competitors provide quick results for their customers: instant access to information, immediate follow-up on requests, and expediting orders.

When there's a problem, they respond quickly. They don't leave the customer hanging. Going to mach one response time means providing customers with the answer, service, information, or solution that they need as quickly as you can. If the customer calls you back for the answer, speed up your response time. Mach one response time is solving problems quickly for customers versus drawing them out.

Attitude drives behavior. If you view serving as a privilege you will naturally seek ways to serve your customers better. Value added peak competitors embrace this attitude. They make it a habit to go the extra mile. They live and work in the proactive mode. They respond quickly to customer requests. They differentiate themselves with their initiative.

Listening to Customers

Everyone wants to believe that they are effective communicators. I've never met anyone who's boasted, "I'm a really poor listener." Listening is a skill. And like all skills, you can improve it.

Active listening is more than hearing or the awareness of sounds. It's inputting verbal and visual cues, processing that information, and attaching meaning to it. It's closing the gap between the sender and the receiver of the message. It's establishing a shared meaning to the sender's message.

Listening to the customer means giving her your full attention. It's avoiding internal and external distractions that often interfere with effective communication. It means listening non-defensively. When a customer calls, it's generally a request for you to solve a problem, not a personal attack directed at you.

I heard this term years ago but don't remember where: naïve listening. This is to listen as a child might. If you have ever told children a story and recall that look on their faces, they listened with wide eyes and open minds. Naïve listening is absorbing information fully and openly, as a child would.

Active listening avoids judging and prejudging people. It's hearing them out fully without allowing your biases to interfere. Active listening requires empathy to understand the feelings behind the facts:

- It's watching for nonverbal clues. It's looking for the consistency between what the customer says and does.

- It's clarifying when you don't understand something that the customer has said.

- It's asking why something is a problem, or how something happened.

- It's restating in your own words to demonstrate that you understand the customer.

- It's listening for the feelings behind the facts.

Listening is especially important when customers just want to vent. They want someone to listen and to demonstrate that they really care what the customer has to say.

Effective communication is necessary for you to do things right the first time, every time, and to avoid mistakes. You must actively listen to the customer's request to provide the right answer. The habit of effective listening means being proactive. When you actively listen to a customer's request or instructions, it helps you to avoid problems in the future.

Active listening demonstrates to other people that you value your relationship with them.

Using your active listening skills internally with your peers, subordinates or internal customers builds stronger teams. It helps you to avoid mistakes. It demonstrates your commitment to the team.

Effective communicators build trust with other people. They listen their way into the hearts of others. To become an effective communicator you must be willing to take a risk. As you listen actively to other people to fully appreciate the meaning behind their words, you risk being changed by the conversation. This is one of the most significant barriers to effective communication. It's difficult for anyone to set aside personal beliefs and prejudices while attempting to understand another person. That's what makes active listening special. Your full concentration and active listening to a peer or customer is an important message. It validates your concern for them while demonstrating your desire to support the relationship.

Chapter Summary

I began and finished this chapter by discussing empathy. I projected you into buying situations where you were treated poorly and treated well to demonstrate how it feels to be the customer. I pointed out that the things that frustrate you as a customer are the same things that irritate your customers. The things that you appreciate and encourage you to return are the same things that your customers appreciate and encourage them to return to your organization.

I discussed your customer value focus. I called it customerizing: understanding the customer's needs from their point of view. It's developing an in-depth understanding of their world from the buyer's perspective. I also discussed the importance of having the attitude of gratitude—that serving is a privilege, not a pain. When the attitude of gratitude is in place, people naturally perform in ways to support that attitude. They take the initiative to go the extra mile. They are proactive in dealing with issues for the customer. They respond quickly to customer's questions and requests. I finished with a discussion on effective communication. What better way to demonstrate empathy for the customer than to listen actively to what they say?

The great challenge in business today is not necessarily to gain new business but to take care of existing customers. It's nailing shut that back door so you don't lose business out of the back door. Too many organizations experience the revolving door syndrome. They lose as much business from the back door as they bring in the front. They have revolving doors on the fronts and backs of their buildings.

As a value added employee, the way you interact with your customers—either directly or indirectly—has a real impact on customer satisfaction, customer loyalty, and customer retention. The ways you approach your job, interact with your peers, and interface with your customers affect the value that your company delivers.

Thought Provokers

- What do your customers have a right to expect from your organization?

- Do you have the attitude of gratitude?

- Are you a good listener?

- How can you better serve your customers?

- Do you view your solution as value received—i.e. do you view it from the customer's point of view?

-6-

After-marketing

In this chapter I discuss after-marketing or defensive selling. This is the sale after the sale. My objective is to involve you and everyone else in your company actively in this defensive sales and service effort. Why? Consider these four studies.

- The data from one study tells us that it costs your company ten times more money to attract new business as it does to serve an existing customer.

- A second study found that two-thirds of the business companies lose every year is because they don't care enough to retain it.

- The third study found that the average U.S. corporation loses half its customer base every five years.

- A fourth study demonstrates that companies lose more business to service complaints than to complaints about their price or their quality.

Tinkering

I begin our discussion on after-marketing with a strategy called tinkering. Tinkering is the behavioral side of that insatiable curiosity about your potential. It results from your productive discomfort with the status quo. To tinker with something is to turn, to twist, and to tweak—to look at something and ask, "What can we do to make this better?" or "How can we make it operate more effectively?" or "How can we bring more value to the customer?"

Tinkering is the habit of continuously looking for ways to recreate value for your customer: every day and in every way we continue to get better.

Tinkering has a long history. The tinkers were a nomadic group of people that lived primarily in Eastern Europe centuries ago. They went from village to village eking out a living repairing tin pots and pans. We believe that's where the word tinkering comes from.

When you tinker with something, you're constantly looking for ways to make it better. Implicit in the definition of tinkering is that you're proactive. You don't wait for customers to initiate these changes. You initiate them.

Am I better off as your prospect or as your customer? Some organizations treat their prospects better than their customers.

Tinkering is treating your customers as if they were prospects—because they are, for the competition. Tinkering is doing what a good, quality competitor does when chasing your business. They ask, "What would you like us to do for you that your current supplier doesn't do?" When you tinker, the fundamental question you ask the customer is, "What do you want us to do for you in the future that we haven't done in the past?"

There are a number of ways to tinker. One, constantly look for ways to build a better mousetrap. Emerson wrote, "If you build a better mousetrap, the world will beat a path to your door to buy it." Tinkering is effective because there's no commodity in creativity. Your creativity coupled with a strong measure of personal initiative expands the gap between your company and the competition.

Tinkering also means barrier analysis and elimination. Examine those barriers that prevent your company from providing the kind of world-class service that you can provide. I touched on this concept in Chapter Two. Look for ways to make it easier for the customer to do business with your company.

One way to tinker is to help your customers become more productive or to achieve more with what you have sold them. Ask, "How can we help this product or service perform better for this customer?" Another way to tinker is to help your customers operate more efficiently, purchase more efficiently, or dispose of a product more efficiently.

To tinker is to satisfy your natural curiosity about your potential. Ask, "How good can we make this?" Every day, in every way, continue to look for ways to get better for the customer and for you. It's pursuing your destiny of growth and development.

Value Reinforcement

The second after-marketing strategy is value reinforcement. Value reinforcement is the sale-after-the-sale. It's defensive selling at its best.

The best defense is a great offense.

Most of the companies with whom I work deliver great value to their customers, but they don't always get credit for it. Because they fail to get credit for it, price is often an issue in the sales process. Value reinforcement is one of the most effective proactive strategies to help customers understand the full value of what you do for them. It helps your company maintain its profitability because you minimize price resistance.

There are a number of ways to use value reinforcement. The first is documentation. Think of some of the value added services that your company delivers and consider some ways to document them.

One idea is the no-charge invoice. The no-charge invoice demonstrates to the customer the dollar value of your service. It quantifies your value added. List the service and its dollar value to the customer. Across the bottom of the invoice, in bold letters type, "Value added services, no charge."

One of my clients invoiced one of their customers for two technical people spending time in the field. They included the travel time, travel expenses, time on the project, and calculated the value of that service. It would have cost the customer $4,400. My client sent that customer a no-charge invoice detailing the nature of the service and the amount of money it would have cost them. On the bottom of the invoice it read, "No charge. Part of our value added service." Until then the customer didn't realize the actual dollar value of the service.

Another one of my clients who sells to a municipality calculated the real dollar value for all of the value added services, replacement products and training that they offered this customer and sent them a series of no-charge invoices.

A purchasing agent from that municipality called the sales rep and thanked him for the no-charge invoices. He liked doing business with this salesperson's company but always felt a lot of pressure from his boss because the supplier charged more than the competition. Now he had the documentation to present to his boss and say, "This is why we're justified in paying their prices. Look at all of this value added!"

Another example is a customer service action report. The customer calls you with a specific problem. On the customer service action report list the situation, your response, and the outcome for the customer. Send them a copy of this report as a post-situation recap. It documents your value added service.

Another of my clients uses a project savings report. When they get involved in a project they calculate the value of their involvement, their dollar impact and send it to the customer, demonstrating their savings.

When you do warranty work for a customer, demonstrate that value with a warranty report. Advise the customer what it would have cost without the warranty support.

Customers that receive complimentary, value added services grow to expect them. This diminishes the perceived value of the services because customers begin to view them as a given.

You can't blame the customer for complaining about price when there's no perceived dollar value for the service that you offer. Your goal is to quantify and communicate the real dollar value to the customer.

You can also use value reminding. Value reminding is a simple but powerful technique of positive bragging. And as Yogi said, "If you're doing it, it ain't bragging." When the customer calls for a specific request that you hand off to someone else, follow-up with the customer to make sure that the customer is satisfied. You know they're satisfied because you've already checked with your peer. But you want the customer to brag about your service.

When you solve a problem for a customer, follow-up with them and ask, "How's that solution working for you?"

Positive bragging puts the spotlight on something that you've done and reinforces it in the customer's mind. Your company is constantly delivering value added to serve them better. That's a great message for the customer to hear.

The value audit is another way to reinforce your value with the customer. It can be as formal as a customer satisfaction survey or it can be as informal as your asking the customer, "How are we performing for you?" Spend time with the customer twice a year and audit your value added services. It's a way to remind them of everything that you do and to check on yourself.

Remember, you can't blame the customer for complaining about price when they're unaware of the real dollar value of the services that you bring to the table.

Value reinforcement works well because the best defense is a great offense. Document your value added. Quantify the value of your services. Make it easy for the customer to justify to themselves and to others why your prices are equitable.

Look for opportunities to brag positively about your service. Put the spotlight on your commitment to serve. Check on yourself often. Ask the customer how you're performing. As they complete your customer satisfaction surveys or answer your questions about your performance, they brag about you while telling you where to improve. Use this information to tinker and to expand the gap between you and your competition. This is real value added.

Relationship Management

Selling is relationship management. How well you manage the relationship determines how long it will last. Relationship building is an important part of after-marketing. This includes all of your efforts to build stronger connections with customers at all levels in the organization.

There are four simple principles for relationship building:

- Number one, trust is the currency of great relationships. When people trust each other, like each other, and want to do business, they will work out the details.

- Number two, the sale must be about the customer, not the seller. Remember, it's their problem, it's their money, and it's a solution with which they must live. The sale must be about the customer. This customer-oriented philosophy has been a central theme throughout this book.

- Number three, customer satisfaction is a function of how your company performs relative to the customer's expectations. If you out-perform their expectations, you have satisfied customers that return with their friends. If you under-perform their expectations, you have dissatisfied customers that do not return.

- Number four, the most important thing to remember in dealing with customers is that it's the customer's perception that ultimately counts. The only reality that matters in business is the reality inside the customer's mind.

You and your peers may believe that your company delivers good service. It's important that you feel this way. But it's imperative that the customer believes it.

These tips will help you build stronger relationships with customers:

- Spend time with your customers and listen more than you talk. That's why you have two ears and one mouth.

- Take a genuine interest in their conversation.

- Perform acts of consideration for the customer.

- Do little things that demonstrate you appreciate their business.

- Use entertainment to build your relationship.

- Look for ways to make your customer a hero.

- Offer preferential treatment to key customers and let them know that they're getting special treatment.

- Involve them in your business. Customer councils, customer feedback sessions, or customer focus groups demonstrate to customers that their input is important to your business.

- Immerse yourself in the customer's business. I've heard countless examples of salespeople that sell through a retail store or outlet, and may spend a weekend day on a special occasion helping that customer. Offer your customers ideas that will help them grow their businesses. Send them customers.

- Look for ways to deliver proactive service. Establish customer loyalty programs that encourage customers to continue to do even more business with you. These are the frequent-buyer programs that motivate customers to increase their routine purchases.

Customer loyalty is a leading predicator of a company's profitability.

You build loyalty as you build the relationship with your customer. This relationship hinges on their trust. Trust results when you put the spotlight on the customer, deliver on your promises, and follow up on their requests.

Customers realize that you're in business to make a profit. When you treat customers as people, not accounts, you demonstrate that you value their relationship as much as you value their business.

Leverage Every Opportunity

Do you know the quickest way for your company to sell more and earn greater profit? Increase your business with existing customers. The quickest way for your company to make more money is to nail shut your back door and increase business with your existing customers. This is leveraging.

Leveraging is achieving a high ratio of outcome to input. It's multiplying your efforts. It's getting a 150% return on a 100% investment. It's selling deeper and broader into your existing base, expanding the depth and breadth of your business.

The average organization can increase its sales by twenty percent in a given year without attracting one new customer if they only did a better job selling to existing customers.

On average, it takes salespeople seven calls to close a new customer on a new idea, yet only three calls to close an existing customer on a new idea. Existing customers buy quicker than prospects, and it costs less to sell more to existing customers.

There are three ways that companies leverage their business. The first is vertical account penetration. This means expanding the mix of your products with a customer, the depth and breadth of what you sell. Some people call this cross selling. It's selling products that automatically create pull for other products. It's expanding the mix of products that you sell.

For example, if you sell industrial equipment, are you getting all the parts business and service work that you should get on the back end? Vertical account penetration is cross-selling additional products and services to existing customers.

There's a practical consideration in leveraging. When a supplier does more business with a customer, the customer is less likely to bounce that supplier when they have a problem. Common sense dictates, if you sell one item to a customer and drop the ball, it's pretty easy for the customer to kiss you goodbye.

On the other hand, if you sell twenty or thirty different items to a customer and have one problem, the customer is not as likely to stop purchasing all thirty of your items because you had a problem in just one area.

Vertical account penetration is reminding customers that you offer additional products and services. Whether you work in the parts department, the service department, customer service, or in sales, remind customers that you sell these other products. They appreciate these reminders and it increases business for your company.

Horizontal account penetration is pursuing business in other locations of existing accounts. In your conversations with customers, ask this question, "Are there other locations that we ought to be talking with?"

Another type of leveraging often goes unrecognized. This is the natural spin-off business you earn from delivering value. "Profit in business comes from customers that are satisfied with your product or service and that return and bring friends with them." (W. Edwards Deming)

Spin-off business results from doing a good job for the customer. They refer others. A customer may say to one of your company's salespeople, "You ought to go talk with so-and-so." Or, the customer tells another person about the great experience they've had. It creates additional demand for your products.

Value added peak competitor organizations maximize their business relationships with customers. They seek ways to expand the depth and breadth of their sales with existing customers.

Put yourself in the customer's shoes. If you're dealing with a supplier that has gone the extra mile, has a customer value focus, and who's interested in making a difference, not just making a deal, aren't you excited enough that you want to tell your friends?

The way you approach your job, the way you interact with your peers, and the way that you approach your customer, affect the spin-off business potential for your company.

Too often, companies explore new business opportunities in different areas when the best opportunities still exist in their own backyards.

Chapter Summary

In this chapter I discussed after-marketing and your personal involvement with customers in this activity. I encouraged you to continue to look for ways to re-create value for the customer and to get credit for all the value that your company delivers. I talked about the importance of building strong relationships with customers. These are relationships that go beyond the product. Loyalty is something we feel toward people, not necessarily toward products. Customers prefer certain products but they feel loyalty to the people from whom they buy. I finished by discussing the importance of leveraging your existing business relationships because it's the quickest and most natural way for your company to increase your business.

Everyone is responsible for sales and service. What would it mean to your organization if everyone embraced the value added philosophy of nailing shut the back door?

I submit that you could lift your company to the next level with your people, not just your products or services. And that's what this book has been about: people adding value to their organization. Your organization is as strong as you are effective. How you perform your job and work with your peers to serve your customers determines the level at which your company competes.

Thought Provokers

- Do we actively seek ways to recreate value for our customers? Are we good tinkers?

- Do we get credit for all of the value added that we bring to the table?

- How can we document our value added?

- How is my relationship with our customers?

- Are we leveraging every sales opportunity?

- How can we increase business with existing customers?

-7-

How to Add Value

This chapter is about everything you've read in The Value Added Organization so far. It serves as a refresher and a primer on how your organization can add more value to your solution. You will see much familiar ground in this chapter as I lay out our models for adding value. This is planned redundancy. Reading only this chapter cheats you out of the entire value added experience contained throughout this book. I suggest that as you read through the examples of value added in this chapter, you build on the concepts not the specific examples. I use the examples to "prime your creativity pump." If you use these examples as a shopping list of things to do, you will have missed the essence of the message. Good luck and enjoy the journey.

Is the Value Added Approach Right For You?

Before launching into a value added business approach you may want to ask yourself this question, "Is this the way for us to compete?" Answering this question before initiating your campaign could save you some major headaches. There are

97

many ways to compete in a market and the value added approach is one of these.

Some companies compete successfully on price. Consider Southwest Airlines, Sam's Wholesale Club, OfficeMax, and Circuit City. They have figured out the economies of scale and the operational efficiencies to make their money on the inside, not the outside.

Other companies compete fiercely because they sell a product that is so desirable that buyers will gladly stand in line and thank the seller for the opportunity of being put on their backorder list—a la Harley Davidson.

If neither of these sound like your company then the value added approach may be the way for your company to compete. This checklist will also help you make that decision:

- You are tired of price objections.
- You are not getting full credit for all the value added your company brings to the table.
- You want to better leverage your significant value added resources.
- You believe this is the most effective way for your company to differentiate itself in your marketplace.
- Your customers are demanding it.
- Your competition is raising the bar.

- You believe that a comprehensive value added solution is the best solution for your customers but have trouble selling this concept to them.

To go into this strategy with your eyes wide open is a good thing. Know this about the value added approach; first, not all customers want it. You will automatically eliminate one out of six buyers for your product or service—they couldn't care less. They are the price segment. Of course, if you want to be known by the company you keep, you probably don't want price-segment business anyway.

Second, many customers will view this approach as nothing more than a marketing cliché. It's not that value added is ho-hum, it's that too many companies have tried to use this approach in the most superficial ways. It's not about smoke and mirrors. It's about creating definable, quantifiable, and meaningful value for the customer. If you want to use the label without the back-end support, save yourself the time and money and save your customers the frustration. Incidentally, in most companies that I work with, the management team cannot detail for me in quantifiable terms their value added proposition.

Third, you will need to develop a communications medium to broadcast to your customers the direct link between your value added and their needs. A failure to explain thoroughly how your value added affects their total cost of ownership and usage will result in missed sales opportunities.

Fourth, on a more positive note, sixty-two percent of your market is so desperate for meaningful value added that they have taken the initiative with their suppliers to encourage them to seek ways to add even more value than they are currently providing. That's an exciting thought.

Characteristics of Value Added Suppliers

Customers have told us what it means to be a value added supplier—distributor or manufacturer. The best of the best share some common denominators. First, they are proactive. This means they stay ahead of the curve with customers. They anticipate and act in advance. They also keep customers ahead of the curve and out of trouble. Working closely with customers for continuous improvement is one of the most proactive ways to re-create value. The best defense is a great offense.

Second, value added suppliers are responsive to customer needs and concerns. If customers have issues, the supplier handles them promptly. Speed and openness characterize this responsiveness. Responsiveness mandates clear, wide, and open communication channels. Management must be accessible to customers.

Third, value added suppliers are relationship-oriented. They value the relationship with their customers as much as they value the business. When products are similar and services converge, relationships may be your only differentiating variable. People like to do business with those they trust.

Fourth, value added suppliers must be empathetic. They must be able to see things from the customer's point of view. Empathy is the primary requirement for a customer value focus.

Fifth, reliability is also high on the customer's list of characteristics for suppliers. Along with responsiveness and trust, customers must feel they can rely on you to deliver on your promises. If they entrust you with business, they want to be able to sleep at night knowing that their goods will arrive on time. The best of the best deliver quality products on time.

Sixth, the fuzziest of these six characteristics is that value added suppliers have the "look and feel" of a company that provides value added services. This "look and feel" reinforces an image in the customer's mind (a.k.a. gut feeling) that they are dealing with a first-class organization. Never underestimate the importance of the intangibles in business.

What Is Value?

Value is often defined in terms of a cost/benefit ratio. Buyers view what they purchase and weigh the outcome of that purchase against what they pay for it. They subtract cost from benefit and anything left is considered value. My definition is a bit more complex yet more descriptive than that. I use a formula:

$$\text{Price} + \text{Cost} + \text{Impact} = \text{Value}$$

Price is the acquisition price. Cost is what it costs the buyer to use, maintain, support, service, and dispose of the product.

Some call this life cycle costing or ownership costs. Impact is the outcome or the effect of the purchase on the customer. This includes direct and indirect benefits of ownership. Impact also includes the ability to do something today that they have not been able to do in the past. For example, if a product gives a distributor the opportunity to pursue a piece of business that they may not have been able to pursue in the past, this has great potential impact on their business. In fact, the greatest value in this last example may be the chance to regain missed opportunities from the past.

So the easy answer to the question, "What is value?" is that value is the *total experience* a customer has with your company and product. Certainly, a company that charges higher front-end prices and delivers even greater value on the back end is a superior buying decision for most customers— except for price shoppers. They only care about the up-front acquisition price.

Buying solely on price is like purchasing a pair of shoes because they fit your budget, not your feet. Wear a pair of cheap shoes that fit miserably for a week and you will curse the day you decided to shop price.

It's the seller's job to convince the buyer that making a decision based strictly on acquisition price is a short-term mistake with long-term and potentially, wide-range consequences. This presumes the seller offers great back-end value.

The Value-add-itude™

It's not a typo. I'm challenging your attitudes toward value. Specifically, from which direction does your definition flow? Are you customer-focused, which means your definition flows from the customer? Or are you seller-focused, which means your definition flows from you to the customer?

Customer-focused definition means that you define value in terms that make sense to your customers. You listen to their needs, wants, and fears and design solutions that fit their definition of value.

Seller-focused value means that you have a menu of "value added" services that you want your customer to buy—whether or not they need or want them. You have something to sell and you want them to buy it. This is a variation of the old Henry Ford-ism, "You can have any car you want as long as it's black."

Some companies call on buyers to create needs while other companies call on buyers to listen to and understand the buyer's needs so that the seller can create a solution. There's a simple principle at work here:

If you define value in customer terms, they pay for it with a higher selling price. If you define value in your terms, you pay for it with a higher discount.

103

From which direction does your definition of value flow? Are you customer-focused in your definition or do you expect the customer to accept your definition of value?

Realities of the Value Added Philosophy

If you want your company to become a value added provider, you must accept some realities. One, value is personal—everyone has his/her own definition of value. Some people define value as the quality of a product or service, quick delivery, available inventory, technical support, or even a cheap price. Like beauty, value is in the eye of the beholder. It's important to believe that what your company sells is a great solution, but to recap a major theme throughout this book, *it ain't value until the customer says it's value.*

Two, if you're committed to becoming a value added organization, you may need to cut some of your value added that is not relevant to the customer and add other value added that they would like to see. The former is especially difficult because there's a good possibility that someone in your company designed this value added, and it's tough to let go of a great idea—especially when it's your own. Somehow it's easier to think that there may be holes or gaps in the value that your company delivers than to accept that your theories of value added may not appeal to your customers.

Three, to design and sell relevant value added you must first learn to think as customers think. In a previous chapter I called this *customer-izing.* View life from their point of view and understand their needs from their perspective. Put yourself in the buyer's shoes and see how they feel. Where do they hurt or pinch? Understand "the look" they're going for. How will they use these shoes—for dancing or for working in the yard? Mostly, define value in their terms. It's their problem. It's their money. It's a solution with which they must live. It should be about them not you.

Four, to sell customer-focused value you must stretch your time horizon and broaden your view of what you sell. Most value added occurs after the sale during usage. Stretch your time horizon and challenge yourself with this question, "How do we bring value to our customers throughout the *entire* buying and usage cycle?" Broaden your view of what you sell. Think beyond your core product. Everything has the seed of a commodity sale, depending on how the seller envisions the solution and describes it to the buyer. This expanded view encourages you to focus on all the reasons why your solution is a great fit for the buyer's needs.

Types of Value

There are two types of value: perceived value and performance value. Perceived value is a promise that you make. It's the sizzle on the steak. It's the gift wrap on the package. It's all the stuff you do that builds customer anticipation and expectations for your solution. This includes packaging, brand name, expertise, reputation, knowledge, etc. These are qualitative examples of how you bring value to the customer. They generally describe who you *are*.

That your organization is a one-hundred-year-old company gives peace of mind to many buyers. They perceive great security in dealing with a centenarian organization. That's the essence of perceived value—it gives your buyer a warm and fuzzy feeling when they buy from you. Much perceived value is sensory: how things smell, taste, look and feel. Packaging is a sensory input stimulus. The buyer processes what that wrapper means to them—they attach a meaning to it—and that is called perception.

Performance value is the proof behind the promise. It's the steak behind the sizzle. It's the gift inside the wrapper. And it's the profit impact you have on the customer's business. Performance value generally includes things like greater efficiency and effectiveness. Giving customers the opportunity to do something they have been unable to do is performance value. These are quantitative examples of how you bring value to the customer. Performance value is what you *do* for the customer.

When your solution helps the customer to use their product more efficiently, manage their people more effectively, or chase a piece of business successfully, you are bringing quantifiable value to the table.

Perceived value may get you the business but performance value brings the customer back—with their friends. Perceived value serves a useful purpose in getting buyers excited. Performance value plays a bigger role in customer satisfaction and retention.

How to Add More Value to Your Solution

If you are a seller-focused organization, I've already described what you do to add value (a.k.a. add cost). You decide what services you want to sell, for whatever reason, and then convince the buyer that they cannot live without them. The focus is on your needs. You may not like that definition, but it's reality.

Customer-focused organizations add value by one of four methods or maybe even a hybrid of them:

Cafeteria-style menu—With this method, the seller presents the buyer with a list of value added services (a master list of everything they offer) that they provide and allow the buyer to pick and choose what they desire. This cherry-pick method lacks an integrated strategy in serving an account, but at least it gives the buyer an opportunity to pay for only that which they feel they can use.

Segment value added—The seller divides his/her market into different segments and establishes a bundle of services that typically appeal to a buyer that fits the parameters of that segment. This may include a high value added segment that requires maximum attention, a medium value added segment that requires much less value, and a low-end price shopper segment that wants it cheap—no value added. This seller has the ability to determine how much time and effort they want to invest in pursuing any of this business.

Process value added—I believe this model holds the greatest promise for most companies. Of the four models I discuss, this is the most customer-centric because it starts with the customer. Ask your buyers this question, "Please walk me through your project or decision process, start-to-finish." This is another way of saying, "How many steps do your buyers go through from the moment that a need exists up to and including using and disposing of the solution that you are attempting to sell them?"

This is a cradle-to-grave analysis of each step on their Critical Buying And Usage Path™, Critical Path™ for short. Every step along this Critical Path™ is an impact area. Your buyer may have as many as a dozen steps along their Critical Path™. The more clearly you identify these steps (i.e. critical impact areas) the more effectively you identify ways that you can add meaningful value. For example, if your buyers have twelve steps along their Critical Path™ (from when the need exists to need satisfaction and disposal) and you offer an average of three value added services at each step along this path, you have thirty-six value adding activities that make up your chronology of value.

This chronology of value is a compelling argument for why the buyer should choose your alternative. Your presentation of this value added sounds like, "Mr. Buyer, we've created a bundle of value added services that supports you from cradle to grave. We know that you will go through these twelve steps in deciding, buying, receiving, using, and disposing of our solution. Our bundle of value supports you at every step along the way..." At this point, use collateral support materials to shore up your argument.

When studying the buyer's Critical Buying And Usage Path™, you will lay out your value added along this path to identify those areas where you add a lot of value added, areas where you offer little or no value added, and areas where you can eliminate some of the value added that you currently offer. This is an effective way for you to assess your total package.

Because the Critical Path™ method is customer-centric, you can offer to do this individually for your top accounts. It provides them with a completely customized solution and it keeps your competitors at bay because you become so thoroughly entrenched.

Category value added—The seller establishes a bundle of value added services that may fit into one of several categories and they present this total package to the customer as justification for their prices. For example, the seller may choose these categories: facilities, technical service department, maintenance and repair, resale and disposal, financing and insurance, logistics support, purchasing systems, or on-site consultation. In designing this list of categories, the seller may have determined that these are the most critical areas in which their customers demand greater value.

This method has advantages because the seller will generally compile this list with the aid of customers. I have used this method in helping manufacturers and distributors gain a deeper understanding of what their market does to add value.

We conduct a value audit of many suppliers or customers in an industry to determine what types of things customers in this market consider to be value added. Once we amass a list of all the examples of value added, we submit this to an analytical procedure called a *content analysis* to determine specific and isolated examples of value added comprising a category.

For example, under facilities, there may be several examples of how a heavy-duty truck dealer adds value: number of locations, convenience of locations, paint shop, lube bay, drivers' lounge, free parking, depth and breadth of inventory, fuel islands, body and frame shop, weekend hours of operation, pump room, etc. Under one category there are eleven specific examples of how this dealer adds value. The category approach provides an effective way for sellers to communicate their value added in sales and marketing.

Your effectiveness in identifying these categories will determine how coherent your message is to the customer. A simple solution is to survey your customers (i.e. those profiled as ideal customers) and ask them to tell you in which areas they want you to concentrate your value added. Measure their responses against your list of value added and see if categories start to emerge.

The Essence of Differentiation

Eighty-two percent of salespeople fail to differentiate their solution from the competition. What are the definable and defendable differences between your company and the competition? Why should someone be willing to spend more money to do business with your company than with the competition? Until your company can successfully answer these questions on the firing line with the buyer, you may be relegated to a me-too status in the buyer's mind.

The value added approach has never been just about beating a competitor. It's more about better serving customers. Value added organizations don't cut the competitor's price, they cut the customer's costs. Value added organizations do not ask, "What do we have to do to beat the competition?" They ask, "What is the most value we can bring to the customer?"

The value added approach is not about beating your competition. That's not your primary mission. Your primary mission is to do a better job for the customer. If you do that, you will beat the competition hands-down, every time. But, you must know what the competition offers. You must study their products, understand their value added, know why their customers love them and are loyal to them, and mostly, know their weaknesses. Chances are, their weaknesses are your strengths and the answer to the question, "What are the definable and defendable differences between you and the competition?"

Examples of Value Added

I debated long and hard with myself whether I should include this section in the book. My fear is that the metabolically-challenged among you (i.e. lazy ones) will take this as your value added list and use it with your customers. But I decided to include this list so that it may stir your creativity and inspire you to pursue your own in-depth value added solutions.

Process value added—Companies that want to use this model will identify critical impact areas along the buyer's Critical Buying And Usage Path™. These steps, albeit generic, are useful for most companies that would like to use this model:

- Sourcing–How do you help the customer understand their needs better and make a good buying decision?

- Acquisition–What do you do to help the buyer place orders?

- Receiving and transitioning–In what ways do you make it easier for the customer to receive your goods, inventory them, and prepare their people and facilities for usage?

- Usage–How does your company help the customer gain maximum performance and economy from your solution?

- Service and maintenance–What do you do to help the customer get service and maintain what you sold them?

- Growth and disposal–In what ways do you help your customer grow, upgrade, and dispose of the solution that they currently have in place?

Using this model helps you understand how your value added supports the customer from cradle to grave. It's also a useful model for communicating your solution.

Category value added—Based on years of research, we have identified twelve primary value added categories. Within each of these categories we have identified about 150 separate examples of how companies add value.

- Planning–This is how a company helps buyers understand their needs, plan their purchase, and source a solution. For example, this might include: formal needs assessment, design assistance and planning, product demonstrations, estimates, etc.

- Acquisition–This is the formal act of placing an order with a supplier and examples of value added may include: electronic commerce (EDI), customized catalogs, fax ordering, purchasing reports, monthly statements versus individual invoices, etc.

- Financing–Some customers need help in arranging for payment. Examples of value added include: flexible payment terms, variable payment schedule, financing assistance with third-party service providers, leasing, rental, customized credit plans, etc.

- Transition—When buyers purchase something new they may need help in preparing their people and facilities for the new purchase. Examples include: training, cross-functional transition teams, installation assistance, facility tours, etc.

- Logistics—This area of value added focuses on the logistical support companies offer: order tracking, just-in-time delivery, free shipping, special packaging, expediting, bar coding, etc.

- Usage—The buyer uses, resells, or transforms your solution into something they can use. Value added includes: performance audits, ongoing training, advertising to create pull, energy audits, inventory management, cost reduction initiatives, etc.

- Maintenance and service—When customers need to maintain what they purchase they look for suppliers that add value like: preventive maintenance, roadside assistance, reminder mailings for service vehicles, loaner equipment, warranty service, etc.

- Customer loyalty programs—This category includes things like: white glove treatment for special customers, gift certificates, customer education programs, customer newsletters, etc.

- Facilities—Some suppliers bring value to the table with their facilities: weekend operations, twenty-four-hour service department, number of locations, specialized repair equipment, etc.

- Personnel–People represent the single, unique dimension of value: twenty-four-hour access to salespeople, knowledgeable staff, product specialists, "S.V.A.T." teams (specialized value added technicians), etc.

- Upgrade and disposal–This category of value added helps customers grow through forward-thinking value added: quick-release on contracts for upgrades, consignment resale, obsolescence protection, economic replacement recommendation, etc.

- Company qualitative–This is a catchall category for everything else that a supplier offers: depth of resources, number of years in business, management philosophy, strategic alliances, etc.

Distributors and Value Added

Distributors enjoy a special relationship with their customers. Current research indicates that customers are relying more on distributors today than they were five years ago. This is a positive trend, and distributors can leverage this relationship as long as they continue to add value, not cost. Every time a distributor touches something it adds cost to the item. Take care to add value with those fingerprints. Dealing with local sources of supply is a real advantage for customers and manufacturers know it. The great battles throughout history were won with superior logistics. Today's business battles are fought with the logistical support of great distribution.

Our research has uncovered a number of prescriptions that customers have written for distributors that want to be known for more than being a satellite warehouse for the manufacturer.

First, the quality addiction is stronger than ever. I found this a bit surprising because I thought that most companies had fixed that problem. Apparently not! My recommendation is to feed the addictive beast. Continue to seek ways to raise the bar on quality. Customers want more of it.

Second, speed rules. Anything you can do to grease the skids and speed up the process will please your customers. Think FedEx. Charge UPS. Less inventory to manage and quicker receipt of goods as they need them pleases customers. They really don't want to be in the logistics business. They view this as your job and will pay for it.

Third, quit thinking about cutting the competition's prices. Concentrate on cutting your customer's costs. Any monkey can sell at a cheaper price. That doesn't take any talent. How can you seriously focus on re-creating value for customers when you spend your time looking over your shoulder at the competition?

Salespeople and Value Added

Salespeople are at least one-third of the value that customers receive—some estimates run higher than that. The same product, from the same company, from two different sales-people is two different solutions. That's why one salesperson can go into a territory and set it on fire. Everyone loves this salesperson, even his manager.

Another sales rep goes into the same territory. He has the same customers, the same product, the same support network, and maybe the same company car. The only difference is the salesperson. One salesperson sets the territory on fire and the other destroys it and the only thing that changed was the salesperson. That's the impact of a salesperson. So how do salespeople bring value to the table?

Having surveyed hundreds of salespeople to identify how they add value, here is a sampling of the list we have compiled to help guide your efforts:

- Conduct a formal needs assessment to help buyers make better decisions.

- Provide hands-on product demonstrations.

- Offer free estimates.

- Help buyers coordinate and direct their resources toward the right solution.

- Confirm order status and follow the supply chain from seller to buyer.

- Provide transitional training for customer employees.

- Give financing assistance.

- Liaison between supplier teams and customer teams.

- Provide guaranteed access twenty-four hours per day.

- Conduct follow-up value audits to ensure that the customer gets all the value added the salesperson promised.

- Offer product performance evaluations.

- Provide resale assistance for used goods.

- Give product pull-through assistance.

- Locate hard-to-find items.

- Arrange for loaner equipment.

- Be an information conduit for the customer and their company for industry trends.

This list is the tip of the value added iceberg. Salespeople bring the most value with their knowledge. Seventy-six percent of the value added that customers receive comes from knowledge-based activities. For salespeople to add value, they must view their role as changing throughout the sales process.

They go from diagnostician to promoter to supporter to customer satisfaction specialist. And they wear many hats: logistics, sales, service, value creation, value reinforcement, and growth specialist.

The question that I like to challenge salespeople with is, "If you were to leave your company tomorrow and go to work for a very good quality competitor, how much business would you take with you?" If the answer is, "Not much," you're not bringing much to the table. If the answer is, "Most of it," you're bringing significant value to the table.

Summary

Becoming a value added supplier means that your organization must be open to creative ways to offer greater value from the customer's point of view. Understand your buyer's definition of value. Add qualitative and quantitative value. Add value by process or by category. Shoot for the gaps in what you offer and what the customer wants and needs. Delete that which is irrelevant to the customer. Get creative and go outside of your industry. Think beyond the generic product and think total solution. And develop a what's-the-most-we-can-do attitude. Remember, your mission is to help your customers become more efficient and effective and to pursue opportunities in the future they have been unable to pursue in the past.

-8-

Where to From Here?

Organizational excellence is the natural outcome of individual and team excellence. The way you approach your career; interact with your peers; and interface with customers determine the level at which your organization competes. Sound familiar? It should. It's been the theme throughout this book. Great organizations are great because of their people. This summary will help you focus in these three areas:

The Way You Approach Your Career

- Take ownership for your career.

- You are responsible for your success.

- Motivation is a do-it-to-yourself kind of thing.

- People work for more than just the money.

- Get curious about your potential.

- Focus on how you add value to your organization.

- Live the value added philosophy in all areas of your life.

The Way You Interact With Your Peers

- Everyone has a customer—internal or external.
- Customer satisfaction reflects employee satisfaction.
- Treat others with respect.
- We is greater than me.
- The way you treat each other in your organization affects how you treat customers.
- Build others up—don't break them down.
- Focus your energy on how you add value to your team.

The Way You Interface With Customers

- Serving is a privilege, not a pain.
- Define value in customer terms.
- Everyone is responsible for customer satisfaction.
- Deliver proactive service.
- Listen more than you talk.
- Seek ways to recreate value for your customers.
- Leverage every opportunity.

I'll end this book the way I began . . .

Do more of that which adds value to your life and less of that which doesn't add value to your day, to your relationships, or to your career.

About the Author:
Tom Reilly

Tom Reilly is president of
Tom Reilly Training, a St. Louis
based company that specializes
in sales and management training.
Tom is uniquely qualified to "lead
the way" because of his outstanding
sales experience, educational back-
ground and success in the training
field. Tom has a master's degree in
Psychology.

Upon graduating from college, Tom went to work for a Fortune 500
chemical company. In his first year he was their top salesman. He
then started his own successful chemical company in Houston, Texas.

In 1981, Tom became a full-time professional speaker and sales
trainer. He has trained more than one hundred thousand salespeople
and sales managers in manufacturing, distribution, and the service
industries. His client list reads like a "Who's Who" in business.

Tom has authored over forty cassette tapes, a video series, and more
than one hundred sales articles. He is also the author of seven hot-
selling books: *Value Added Selling, Value Added Sales Management,
Value Added Customer Service, Simple Psychology, Selling Smart!,
Crush Price Objections,* and *The Value Added Organization.*

Books and Tapes by Tom Reilly

Not all readers are leaders, but all leaders must be readers. (Harry S Truman)

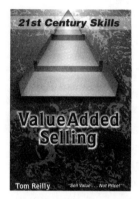

Value Added Selling
The 21st Century Advantage

by Tom Reilly

Value Added Selling is a content-rich message of hope. Whether you're an experienced veteran or a wet-behind-the-ears rookie, you will find this proven customer-oriented sales philosophy a breath of fresh air. It's built on a very simple yet profound truth: you can compete successfully and profitably without being the cheapest. **Value Added Selling** teaches you how to sell value, not price. This is the book that launched the value added selling revolution in the 1980's and has been rewritten in 2000 for the twenty-first century. This twenty-six-chapter book offers an in-depth explanation of the value added sales process. It is divided into four sections:

- Section One–Introduction to the value added sales philosophy and what buyers really want from suppliers;

- Section Two–The strategic side of **Value Added Selling**: eleven strategies that value added salespeople use to identify, penetrate, capture, and retain profitable business;

- Section Three–The tactical side of **Value Added Selling**: how to plan and execute the value added sales call;

- Section Four–Bonus section on selling to high-level decision makers, technology, sales letters, and value added time management.

Book: $24.95   ISBN: 0944448-18-6

Six-audio cassette album: $65.00   ISBN: 0944448-15-1

Order from your local bookstore or online from Amazon.com

Contact us: 1-800-727-0026   **www.tomreillytraining.com**

Crush Price Objections

Hold the line on prices!

by Tom Reilly

If you're fed up with price resistance, this book is for you. If you want to sell at higher prices, this book is for you. If you want to persist when they resist, this book is for you. This practical street-smart, how-to guide is for anyone that sells in a price-sensitive market. It's divided into three parts:

- Part One—Preparing to sell in a price-sensitive market;

- Part Two—Proactive selling: how to avoid price objections;

- Part Three—How to respond effectively to price objections and negotiate better deals.

Book: $19.95   ISBN: 0-944448-14-3

Two-audio cassette album: $20.00   ISBN: 0944448-16-X

Order from your local bookstore or online from Amazon.com

Contact us: 1-800-727-0026   www.tomreillytraining.com

Value-Added Sales Management

A Guide for Salespeople and Their Managers

How to Get More Sold—
Profitably, Confidently,
and Professionally

TOM REILLY

Value Added Sales Management

Building the Value Added Sales Culture

by Tom Reilly

Sales managers are the change agents for their sales organizations yet most of them are woefully unprepared for the challenge. **Value Added Sales Management** is a comprehensive guide for sales managers—new or experienced. In this book, Tom Reilly shares his insights on having trained more than one hundred thousand salespeople and their managers. Reilly's motto is simple: "Manage the process and lead your people." He focuses on the critical dynamics of how managers create the value added sales culture and unleash the potential of their sales forces:

- Management and leadership;
- Selection techniques for hiring the best;
- Training and development;
- Establishing sales objectives;
- Coaching for high performance;
- Compensation trends and strategies;
- Motivating plateaued salespeople.

Book: $12.95   ISBN 0-8092-3787-3

Order from your local bookstore or online from Amazon.com

Contact us: 1-800-727-0026   www.tomreillytraining.com

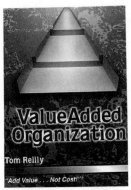

The Value Added Organization

by Tom Reilly

Organizational excellence is the natural outcome of individual and team excellence. Tom Reilly recorded this facilitator-driven, in-house, six-videocassette training series to help organizations introduce their employees to the value added philosophy. The total running time for all six videos is two hours and ten minutes. This translates into nine hours of training and discussion for your employees on how your organization can become a real value added organization. These are some of the important themes covered in this program:

- You and your career: how do you personally add value to your organization's solution?
- You and your peers: how do you add value to your team?
- You and your customers: how do you add value to your relationships with your customers?
- Simply, the way you approach your career, interact with your peers, and interface with your customers determines the level at which your organization competes.

Video series: $600.00 (USD)   ISBN: 0944448-17-8

Book: $10.00   ISBN: 0944448-19-4

Order from your local bookstore or online from Amazon.com

Contact us: 1-800-727-0026   **www.tomreillytraining.com**

Value Added Customer Service

The Employees Guide for Creating Satisfied Customers

by Tom Reilly

Customer service is more than a department. It's the attitude that everyone is responsible for customer satisfaction. **Value Added Customer Service** promotes a simple philosophy of exceeding customer expectations and a positive attitude toward serving customers: serving is a privilege, not a pain. In a fiercely competitive world, closing the deal is only part of the solution. Companies that focus on satisfying customers after the sale increase customer loyalty and retention. Those who fail to provide Value Added Customer Service scramble to recover the business they lose every year to customer defections. If zero defects is a product quality standard that you aspire to then zero defections must be a customer retention standard that you live by. Here are some of the topics covered in this book:

- Who is responsible for customer satisfaction? Everyone;
- The barriers to effective serving;
- The importance of internal customer service;
- How to deliver Value Added Customer Service.

Book: $12.95   ISBN 0-8092-3190-5

Order from your local bookstore or online from Amazon.com

Contact us: 1-800-727-0026   www.tomreillytraining.com

Simple Psychology

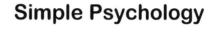

Simple Living in a Complex World

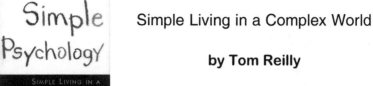

by Tom Reilly

Everyone craves simplicity and balance in their complicated lives. **Simple Psychology** is a breath of fresh air in a world crowded with a misery of choices and obligations. It's a return to the values you learned a long time ago and know that ultimately matter. **Simple Psychology** offers spiritual fuel and emotional salve while challenging you to reflect on the choices that you make and how they affect your life and those whom you love. It encourages you to focus on your "being" versus your "having". These are a few of the essays that appear in this book:

- Success is the quality of your journey;
- Can I make a difference?
- Positive mental programming;
- Burdens and blessings;
- Gifts of time.

Book: $19.95   ISBN 0-944448-11-9

Order from your local bookstore or online from Amazon.com

Contact us: 1-800-727-0026   **www.tomreillytraining.com**

Selling Smart

Great Thoughts for Salespeople

by Tom Reilly

Knowledge is power and since 1981 Tom Reilly has been empowering salespeople and their managers with his ideas. Tom has written over one hundred articles for sales, management, and customer service. Tom has selected fifty-nine of his favorites and assembled them in book form. He offers his thoughts in these areas:

- Communications;
- Time management;
- Value Added Selling;
- Attitude;
- Customer service.

Book: $11.95   ISBN 0-944448-09-7

Order from your local bookstore or online from Amazon.com

Contact us: 1-800-727-0026   **www.tomreillytraining.com**